POPE INNOCENT III AND HIS TIMES

By
Joseph Clayton. F.R. Hist. S.

With a New Introduction by:
PHILIP CAMPBELL
Author of the "Story of Civilization" and other works

MEDIATRIX PRESS

MMXVI
http://www.mediatrixpress.com

ISBN-10: 1535231610
ISBN-13: 978-1535231619

Nihil obstat:
H. B. Ries,
Censor librorum

Imprimatur: ✠ Moyses E. Kiley,
Archiepiscopus Milwaukiensis
December 13, 1940

Originally published by
The Bruce publishing company, 1941.

©Mediatrix Press, 2016
www.mediatrixpress.com
This book may not be reproduced for commercial purposes whether in electronic or physical format, and may not be reproduced as a whole without the explicit permission of the publisher.

Fell Fonts are digitally reproduced by Igino Marini, www.iginomarini.com. Used with permission.

Table of Contents

The Life and Times of Lothario de Conti of Segni
Phillip Campbell. xi

AUTHOR'S PREFACE. xxiii

CHAPTER I

> Twelfth-Century Christendom . . . The "Golden Age of Europe"—Intellectual Renaissance—Empire Versus Papacy—Problems of Feudalism—The Crusades—Witness of Sanctity... 1

CHAPTER II
> Lothario Conti
> Youth and Student Years—Paris—Law Studies at Bologna—False Decretals—Canon Law and Christian Marriage—Cardinal Deacon—Three Treatises—Pope Innocent III.. 19

CHAPTER III
> Pope Innocent III
> Consecration and First Sermon—Judge in the Supreme Court—Central Europe and the near East—Gerald of Wales and Pope Innocent.. 39

CHAPTER IV
> City of Rome and States of the Church
> Conflicts Within Rome—anti-papal Forces—innocent's Services to Rome—hospital of the Holy Spirit—states of the Church—kingdom of the Two Sicilies.. 63

CHAPTER V
> Pope Innocent and the Empire
> Imperial Throne Vacant—Rival Emperors— Innocent Supports Otto of Brunswick—Otto Sole Emperor — Hostility in Rome—Otto Excommunicated —Election of Frederick II.. 83

CHAPTER VI
> Pope Innocent and the Crusades
> Fourth Crusade—Diversion to Constantinople—Sack of Constantinople—The Children's Crusade.. 105

CHAPTER VII
> The Latin Empire of the East
> No Stable Foundation—Innocent's Conciliatory Policy—War with Bulgarians—Death of Baldwin—Feuds of Franks and Venetians.. 123

CHAPTER VIII
> Albigensian and Other Heresies in the West
> Nature of Catharist or Albigensian Dogma—Its Wide Acceptance in Southern France—Support of Count Raymond VI of Toulouse—Innocent's Missionaries—Arrival of Dominic and Bishop Diego—Murder of Papal Legate—Crusade Against the Albigenses—Overthrow at Battle of Muret—Franciscan Antidote to Waldensian Heresy—Abbot Joachim of Flora.. 133

CHAPTER IX
> Relations with England
> Vacancy at Canterbury—Stephen Langton—Interdict and Excommunication—Feudatory of the Pope—Magna Carta.. 161

CHAPTER X
>Fourth General Council of the Lateran
Constitution of the Council—Canons of the
Council—Relics and Indulgences—The Jewish Question.
.... 177

CHAPTER XI
>The Passing of Pope Innocent.................. 197

Table of Dates. 204

Notes on Authorities............................... 205

To
The Dear Memory of
Father Bede Jarrett, O.P., S.T.L., M.A. (Oxon)
obiit March 17, 1934

Dilectus Deo et hominibus, cujus memoria in benedictione.

The Life and Times of Lothario de Conti of Segni
Phillip Campbell

IN THE LONG HISTORY of the Catholic Church, 266 men have sat upon the throne of St. Peter. Most have been unremarkable, no better or worse than any other pastor. Of many we know very little save their pontifical names and regnal dates. Some, of course, have been scoundrels – and what exactly constitutes a "bad pope" has been discussed intensely amongst the devout, especially in recent years. A modest number of popes have been truly great men, and some of them even saintly. As of 2016, the Church recognizes 81 popes as saints. Close to 40% of these, however, are venerated by virtue of a martyrdom, not necessarily because of their personal holiness.

But even among the popes who were truly great or saintly, there is a still smaller subcategory: popes who have been so influential as to define or shape the character of the age in which they lived. Pope Innocent III, the subject of this work, undoubtedly belongs to this category, and in his company are very few others; perhaps only St. Gregory the Great, St. Gregory VII, and Bl. Pius IX stand in his illustrious company.

To say Innocent III epitomizes the character of the age is no overstatement. He is frequently cited in medieval textbooks as the exemplification of a powerful papacy at the height of its temporal influence. His teachings on the relation between the *sacerdotium* and *imperium* summarize the best of the medieval tradition, often referred to as the Two Sword theory (cf. Luke 22:38), where the two swords held by St. Peter represent the temporal and spiritual authority, both of which are in the keeping of the Church – though one is delegated to the state. In his actions in relation to the great figures of his time, Pope Innocent III is the dominant figure, determining the direction of Christendom by his assent or dissent. He received England as a feudal fief from King John, bartered with the patrimony of the Hohenstaufen emperors to strengthen the power of the Church, summoned crusades, chartered the University of Paris, gave the world the Franciscan Order, and called the greatest ecumenical council of the Middle Ages. His very life and thought characterized the 13th century.

Innocent III began life as Lothario de Conti. Like many important ecclesiastics of his day, Lothario born into the nobility around 1160. He was the son of Count Trasimund of Segni, a fortified city not far from Rome in the Papal States. Lothario's family had close connections to papal court. Lothario was the nephew of the future Pope Clement III through his mother's side; in the 13th century two more popes, Gregory IX and Alexander IV, would come from the Conti.

The medieval counts of Segni were stalwart defenders of the papacy, the city often having served as a place of refuge for the popes in times of turmoil. When Lothario was a boy, the greatest site in Segni would have been the new papal palace, constructed during the pontificate of Eugenius III (1145-1153), only a decade or so before Lothario's birth. Given its status as a stronghold of papal support, it was fitting that the cathedral of Segni be chosen as the site for the canonization of St. Thomas Becket, which Alexander III performed in 1173. We are not certain, but it is reasonable to assume the young Lothario was in attendance that day, perhaps already in Minor Orders.

We do not know whether Lothario had other brothers, but it seems that he was a younger son, as he was destined for the

Church at a young age, a common vocation for the younger sons of the medieval nobility. Count Trasimund sent the young boy to Rome for studies, and then on to Paris where he completed his theological training. At the time young Lothario arrived at Paris, the famous University of Paris was still nominally attached to the cathedral school at Notre Dame. It is one of the great ironies of history that years later it would be Innocent III himself who would officially recognize Paris as an independent University in the year 1200.

At Paris, Lothario studied under some of the greatest theological minds of the 12th century, including Peter of Poitiers, Melior of Pisa, and Peter of Corbeil. However, it was not the science of theology that would unlock Lothario's talents, but jurisprudence. After some time at Paris, Lothario returned to Italy to study law at the famous University of Bologna. We spoke earlier of the pontificate of Innocent III characterizing the age in which he lived. This is especially true with relation to canon law, the discipline that was to propel Lothario de Conti to the highest office in the Church.

An aside upon the development of canon law is necessary here. The full deposit of Divine Revelation came through the person of Christ to the Apostles. But as the Church grew, it was only natural that the increasing demands of a bigger and more complex organization required the institution of certain disciplines for the sake of maintaining order and preserving the apostolic traditions. These disciplines were often formulated in response to questions on the practicalities of Christian life: How long should a man be baptized before he presents himself for ordination? What penance is proper for a repentant apostate? If pagans convert to the faith, how was one to discern which of their many customs were compatible with Christianity and which must be repudiated?

The disciplines inaugurated in response to these challenges were early on given the name *canons,* from a Greek word meaning "measure"; that is, one's conduct measured up to the Christian Gospel to the degree that it conformed to the accepted disciplines. From the earliest days of the Church, it was common for both regional synods and ecumenical councils to put their judgments into action by issuing canons, which were binding disciplines upon the faithful either of a region (in the case of a synod) or the entire Church (in the case of an ecumenical council).

As centuries passed and the Church spread, it became customary to consult the canons for guidance in what to do in particular situations. It was a very natural Catholic impulse: to interpret the new in light of the old. But sometimes there were so many canons on a particular question, it was difficult to understand what represented the tradition of the Church. Or sometimes newer canons had tended to replace older ones without the older ones having been explicitly repealed, which meant the existence of simultaneously contradictory canons. In addition to this, different regions or populations often had different customs, which was not an issue when the populations remained relatively homogenous. But it did become problematic when migrations or conquests resulted in mixed populations with mixed customs.

The Normans in particular frequently brought this problem into the fore. When a horde of French-Norman warriors in the service of William of Normandy conquered Anglo-Saxon England, how would Norman ecclesiastical customs integrate with older, Saxon usages? When the Normans conquered Sicily, they imposed Norman ecclesiastical customs on the Greek Christians they found there, prompting the Greeks to complain to Constantinople and beginning a dispute that led to the mutual excommunications of 1054.

There are many other examples, but the point is that by the high Middle Ages, it was often a very confusing thing to sort out exactly what the prevailing custom was. This led to the rise of the canonist movement in the 11th-13th centuries. The canonist movement was prompted by the rediscovery of the ancient *Coprus Iuris Civilis* of Justinian I in northern Italy sometime around 1070. Why the old codex of Justinian suddenly reemerged in the late 11th century is a matter of historical debate; some suggest it was uncovered as part of the inquiries of the Gregorian Reform, which had emphasized canonical studies.

At any at rate, the *Corpus Iuris Civilis* sparked a revival in the study of canon law, its center being the northern Italian city of Bologna, where a university was established devoted to its study. It was from Bologna that the Camaldolese monk known as Gratian studied canon law, going on to compose his famous *Decretals* around a decade before the birth of Lothario. The *Decretals* were to canon law what Aquinas' *Summa Theologica* would become to theology. The *Decretals* were a collection of canons dealing with almost every aspect of ecclesiastical discipline. The texts of the *Decretals* were often formulated in the context of "difficulties", where discordant canons were presented and doubts were raised about their application. Gratian would then propose "distinctions", considerations drawn from canonical history, that helped reconcile the divergent canons. Gratian's work would become the point of reference for all future canonical studies, retaining a place as the norm for canonical interpretation until the promulgation of the 1917 Code of Canon Law. Armed with Gratian's *Decretals* and a fiery zeal, the 12th century canonists of Bologna labored for the better organization and more efficient management of the Church according to the holy canons.

When Lothario entered the University of Bologna, Gratian's *Decretals* were already being studied assiduously by the Church's canonists. We may assume that young Lothario spent hours poring over the writings of Gratian, noting the difficulties Gratian proposed, and committing the hundreds of distinction to memory. His work was well rewarded; Lothario earned a reputation as one of the most skilled canonists at the University.

Bologna was not the only center of the canonist movement. In Rome, the papal throne had been long held by Alexander III, himself a renowned canonist. In fact, had the Church never had Innocent III, history would probably have settled on Alexander III as the greatest canonist-pope of the Middle Ages. Alexander had a troubled pontificate, but he remained a devoted canonist and made several important contributions to the Church's canonical disciplines. His most notable contributions in this regard were his decree vesting the sole rights of papal elections in two thirds of the Cardinals, as well as his formal standardization of the canonization process. Under Alexander III, the canonist movement became papal policy throughout the Church.

We have mentioned that the family of Lothario de Conti were close to the papal court. The eye of the great canonist pope Alexander could not have failed to take note of the young protégé of Bologna. Alexander died in 1181, however, prompting the summons of Lothario from Bologna to Rome where he held a variety of increasingly important ecclesiastical posts. He advanced rapidly through the short pontificates of Alexander's successors. Providence again smiled on him when his uncle Paolo Scolari was elected Clement III in 1187. Clement made Lothario a Cardinal-Deacon in 1190, elevating Lothario to the cardinalate and admitting him to the circle of the *papabile*.

However, in 1191 his kinsman died and Celestine III ascended to the Chair of Peter. Celestine was of the house of Orsini, traditional enemies of the counts of Segni. Seeing his ecclesiastical career at a temporary dead end, Lothario withdrew from Rome to the district of Anagni and devoted himself to writing. During this period he probably composed his famous *De miseria humanae conditionis* ("On the Misery of the Human Condition"). The work is a meditation on the brevity and sorrows of human life and an exhortation to prepare oneself for the kingdom of heaven.

Cardinal Lothario's exile went on for seven long years, and at the time may have seemed permanent. By 1198 the health of Celestine III was failing (he was 92 years old), but he was canvassing the cardinals to vest their support in Giovanni de Colonna (the Colonna had at that time not yet inaugurated their famous feud with the Orsini). With the death of Celestine imminent, Lothario returned to Rome to participate in the impending papal conclave. Pope Celestine expired on January 8, 1198; with his dying wishes he had commended Giovanni de Colonna to the cardinals, but the cardinalate rejected the dead pope's wishes and selected Cardinal Lothario de Conti. The votes in favor of Lothario were strong; he was elected January 8, 1198, the very day Celestine died.

Further testimony to the confidence of the cardinal electors in Lothario's suitability for the papal throne can be deduced from his age. At the time of his election, Lothario was 37 years old, making him the youngest man ever elected pope.

Accounts say Lothario accepted the tiara with reluctance. Of course, every pope or monarch traditionally feigns reluctance when assuming power, but in the case of Lothario we have no reason to suspect it was feigned. He had been out of favor with the papal court for seven years. The powerful Orsini pope had already identified a successor hostile to his family. Lothario's reputation was as a scholar and canonist, not a flatterer, power-broker, or sycophant. When Lothario retired to Anagni in 1191, there is no reason to suspect he ever entertained aspirations to the papal throne, much less anticipated his elevation when entering the conclave on January 8, 1198 at such a young age.

Lothario took the regnal name Innocent III. Why did

Lothario choose this nomenclature? Pope St. Innocent I was a 5th century pontiff from the reign of Emperor Honorius. More likely, Lothario had in mind the more recent Pope Innocent II (r. 1130-1143). Innocent II had a very troubled papacy. From the moment of his election in 1130, his pontificate had been plagued by a schism centered on the claims of antipope Anacletus II, a schism that rent Christendom and required the diplomacy of none other than St. Bernard of Clairvaux to resolve. Besides ecclesiastical divisions, Innocent II had struggled valiantly – but ultimately in futility – against aggression from a host of temporal lords: King Roger II and Roger III of Sicily, Louis VII of France all variously opposed him; as he lay dying, even the Roman people rose up against him in the person of Arnold of Brescia and the Commune of Rome. Innocent II had been a pope who had struggled to strengthen the independence of the papacy in Italy and abroad and had faced innumerable setbacks. Perhaps in the choice of his name, Lothario de Conti signified his resolution to carry on the mission of his predecessor in establishing a respected, independent papacy.

The new pontiff certainly had a daunting task ahead of him. It is beyond the scope of this introduction to go into all of the acts of Innocent III; the book will do that well enough. It suffices to say that Lothario proved to be a pope of astounding energy and vision. He also inherited all the political problems that had plagued the occupants of the throne of Peter for the past century and a half. Though the Investiture Controversy had formally ended over seventy-five years earlier with the Concordat of Worms, the relationship between the papacy and the temporal powers of Europe remained a hotly contested issue, especially in Italy and the Holy Roman Empire. Innocent would become deeply embroiled in the politics of the empire as the godfather of Frederick II Hohenstaufen, grandson of Holy Roman Emperor Frederick Barbarossa. From the very beginning of his papacy his relation to the future Holy Roman Emperor would have drastic implications for papal diplomacy in Sicily and Italy.

Within the Empire, Innocent was able to exploit the schism caused by a contested imperial election to reaffirm the traditional right of the papacy to crown the Holy Roman Emperor. The politics of the Holy Roman Empire in the 13th century were split between two parties, the pro-papal Guelphs, and the pro-imperial Ghibellines. In the contest imperial election of 1198 – only three months after Innocent's elevation to the papacy – the new pope sympathized with the Guelph candidate Otto IV over the Ghibelline Philip of Swabia. The party of Philip resented what they perceived as Innocent's unwarranted interference in the affairs of the Empire. Innocent responded with his first magisterial teaching, the decree *Venerabilem*.

Venerabilem was a hugely important document, not only in the papacy of Innocent but in the development of canon law; the decree was later incorporated into the Corpus Iuris Canonici. The *Venerabilem* encapsulates the entire medieval theory of the *translation imperii*. This was the idea that the imperial power was "transferred" from the Greeks to the Germans. This right to the imperial power was granted the Germans by the Apostolic See, when the pope conferred the imperial crown upon Charlemagne. The right to investigate and decide whether a king thus elected is worthy of the imperial dignity belongs to the pope, whose office it is to anoint, consecrate, and crown him – or to refuse such if he deems in unworthy of the imperial dignity.

The decree was received with submission by many German princes, although the irascible nature of Otto ultimately led support to sway to Philip.

One of the things for which Innocent III is most well known is his connection to the most renowned Catholic Saint—whose appeal crosses confessional and even religious lines—namely St. Francis of Assisi.

Francis, finding himself at the head of a group of men that wished to throw off the world as even he had, sought ecclesiastical approval. For this he ventured to meet the Pope, our Lothario, to beg his approval. The Innocent was impressed by Francis, but leaned to those Cardinals who felt the order was too austere. As the biographers of St. Francis tell it, Innocent had a dream where he saw the church of the Lateran falling down and it was Francis who held up the Church. After this, Innocent hearkened unto the counsel of Cardinal Ugolino (his nephew and the future Pope Gregory XI), as well as the Bishop of Assisi and gave Francis his approval. Given that Innocent was committed to the reform and renewal of the Church in every way, it is only fitting that he should have been the one to approve St. Francis, whose life, example and order would serve so well to build up and reform the Church in those times. In Francis he recognized a mighty adversary to the vices of the age, above all luxury and indolence on the part of both clergy and laity. What Innocent III accomplished in the political and canonical life of both Church and State was wonderfully perfected in the spiritual and pastoral life of both through St. Francis.

The crown of Innocent's pontificate, however, was his accomplishment of the Fourth Lateran Ecumenical Council. He had meant to call a Council since the beginning of his pontificate, but was only able to bring it into being at the end. In his bull of April 19, 1213, Innocent arranged for the Council to meet two and a half years later, in November of 1215. This decision had the happy result of attendance by a large number of Bishops, as well as Patriarchs from Antioch and Alexandria, as well as what was at that time the Latin Patriarchate of Constantinople and envoys from every major monarch in Europe. The Council pronounced several doctrines, in which the word *Transubstantiation* makes its first appearance in magisterial teaching. It also initiated numerous reforms in Canon Law and Ecclesiastical discipline. The Council was the crowning event of this titanic Pope's ceaseless energy to reform the Church and protect her independence from the secular power. His death the next year left behind a legacy of zeal for reforming the Church's life and renewing her institutions.

AUTHOR'S PREFACE

EVERY country has its statesmen, every people its heroes, and its heroines. History sifts the claims to greatness and in each nation distinguishes the demagogue, the charlatan—the popular figure of the day—from the statesman. It does the same with literature. The writer of the "best seller" passes into oblivion, while the talent of authors little recognised in their age may receive ample acknowledgement from later generations. "The whirligig of time brings in its revenges."

We cannot know too much of the statesman who has faithfully served a nation, and no nation can have too many such men rightly honoured. Centuries cannot wither the laurels that crown the true statesman's life, his fame is assured whilever the love of people for their country endures. Pope Innocent III was the greatest statesman Europe has known. He stands apart from all statesmen who have laboured—frequently in devious ways, seeing no other—to do the best for their country, indifferent to the welfare of other nations.

Pope Innocent III was, first and last, the statesman of the medieval Europe we call Christendom. Elected pope, he saw himself as Christ's vicar, God's viceroy in the Kingdom of God on earth, to whom had been committed the care of all the churches, the well-being of all nations in that very limited world of the Middle Ages. It was not quite all Europe. On the eastern frontiers stood Russia, the country of the Muscovites, while heathenism still flourished in Baltic lands. Only a fringe of Asia was Christian, the greater number of its inhabitants adhering to the rule of Constantinople rather than that of Rome, and living under threat of destruction by militant advancing hosts of Islam. No part of Africa now retained the faith, for the Arabs held all the northern lands, while the once glorious church of St. Augustine and St. Cyprian was long extinguished. The Europe included under the cross extended from Scandinavia to Spain, and from Ireland and Great Britain on the west to Bohemia and Hungary on the east. It was a Europe distracted in every century of the Christian era by the ambitions of rulers and rent by conflicts; a Europe, nevertheless, that in spite of wars and rumours of war, saw the building of cathedrals and abbeys, marvellous in their beauty, and felt the thirst for learning that sent youth in thousands to Paris and Bologna, thence to Oxford and elsewhere; a Europe that in its houses of religion produced the overwhelming holiness of St. Bernard, that drew St. Dominic from his cathedral canonry and St. Francis from exuberant civic life to send forth their sons to evangelise the world.

This was the Europe, at the climax of its medieval renaissance, that Innocent III was called to shepherd, to guide, to exhort, and, as its spiritual father, to govern. Ancient communities of Christians in India, in Abyssinia, and Syria, long cut off from all communication with the Christendom of Europe, grew up outside the unity and government of the Catholic Church that had its centre in Rome.

Trained in the art and science of government by an early call to the papal court, yet never a bureaucrat who sacrificed his manhood to officialdom; skilled in the knowledge of law, yet never allowing the legal mind to function at the expense of the love of his neighbour; claimed by the active life that denied leisure for the purely contemplative, yet always living as the servant of God, as the *servus servorum Dei* (slave or servant of the servants of God), Innocent III unhesitating, unresting, fought the good fight, finished his course. Prepared to adjust and, if necessary, change political plans, he was no mere doctrinaire in things temporal, being the true statesman fully aware that there is a time for expediency, but always insistent on the supremacy of the moral law. A lover of order and the paths of peace, with the knowledge that on occasion the pride of unruly princes can be curbed by the power of the sword alone, and so peace and order be assured to the multitude — Pope Innocent III remains the great example of Christian statesmen — pre-eminently Christian because he had neither army nor navy to enforce his authority. His sovereignty was a spiritual authority, his kingdom the kingdom of God and his Christ.

The difficulties confronted by Innocent in the years when he reigned were stupendous, incessant the conflicts. The difficulties and conflicts endure. For the same two questions that demanded answer in the Middle Ages, and that if left unanswered brought great tribulation, now again press for answer in our own day.

1. Is there a moral law divinely appointed for all mankind?
2. Is there a supreme spiritual voice to declare to all mankind the moral law of God, a spiritual authority divinely contrived to counsel the troubled and guide the stumbling steps of wayfaring men?

On the answer to these questions depend both present and future hopes, and the success or failure of the best-laid plans of men and women of good will.

This is but a short survey of the life and times of Innocent III—though its preparation has meant long study. It may perhaps stimulate the reader to pursue the subject and gain further knowledge by consulting some of the books mentioned in the text and named at the end. Recalling the past and giving praise to famous men, our fathers who begot us, we can at least face the more courageously the problems of our own day, the problems that beset mankind in every age of this earthly pilgrimage.

Fidelity to truth is the first and last obligation of the

historian. Disloyalty to truth his deepest treachery. The chronicler collects the facts and sets them out. The writer of history must do more than that. He must find out the meaning and significance of the facts and correlate them. The *how* and the *why* of the course of human events are the business of the historian, and being mortal he may err in the interpretation of human motives — so rarely single are the purposes of a man's acts; so frequently diverse, so unexpected, the results. But to let malice, prejudice, or sheer ignorance burke the evidence, thwart the reasoned judgement, or permit suppression of truth that is disagreeable to settled opinions, to long-cherished habits of mind, is the unpardonable sin.

"Truth has many admirers but few servants" wrote Cardinal Newman's friend and fellow Oratorian, Father Dudley Ryder. The author of this small contribution to the study of a very great and good man and his times would ask to be remembered with the few; for he has sought to serve truth, the whole truth, and nothing but the truth in the pages that follow.

J. C.

Chipping Campden,
Glos., England.

Pope Innocent III and His Times

CHAPTER I
Twelfth-Century Christendom

> Twelfth-Century Christendom ... The "Golden Age of Europe"—Intellectual Renaissance—Empire Versus Papacy—Problems of Feudalism—The Crusades—Witness of Sanctity.

WHEN Pope Celestine III died at the age of ninety-one and his successor, Lothario Conti, on election to the papacy became Pope Innocent III, the great twelfth century was near its end. It was the century of vital issues, of revival in intellectual conflict, of rebirth of learning, of an enthusiasm for study such as Europe had never before known; a century pre-eminent in the history of Europe, famous for all time in the history of Christendom; a century not only of mental strife but of saints and statesmen profoundly influencing their age and the ages to come. From without, the Christendom of Europe was threatened by the growing power of Islam, from within by the disintegrating and increasing activity of the sect of Catharists whom we know as Albigenses. Constantly distracted, too, was that Christendom by the claims of powerful emperors, looking back to the heroic figure of Charlemagne, while seeking supreme rule over the Catholic Church and wishing to set up in Rome itself a pope obedient to imperial policy. The decisive question—who was the real head of Christendom, pope or emperor?—was hotly and violently disputed, nor could it be settled as the emperors would have it. Feudalism added to the difficulties, for without the feudal law how could armies be enrolled and wars waged?

And while scholars and students crowded to find learning, while saints and statesmen laboured to bring people to God and to establish submission to law, while the armies of kings and emperors tramped their destructive way across Europe, the common people in every land sought peace. All they wished for was to sow the land and till it. It was a hard time for the peasantry, that golden middle age of the twelfth century, for on them in their serfdom fell the burden both of military service to their feudal lord and of raising food. And the centuries to come brought slow enfranchisement. Yet the peasant's son, however hard his lot, was not excluded from the fellowship of learning. Touched by the spirit of understanding that moved uncounted thousands in Europe, he felt the enkindling love of study and of religion, and would not be hindered from seeking a scholar's life at one of the new universities or admission at the monasteries then rising in such numbers over France and England. In Rome itself a peasant's son could be chosen to be pope, as was Hadrian IV, the only Englishman elected to the throne of St. Peter.

How can we account for that marvellous revival of learning in the twelfth century or explain the rise of the university? No one man or group of men can be named. All that historical research can do is to reveal to us ardent youthful minds receptive to teaching, zealous men of brilliant intelligence willing to impart and expound. This also can be said; the cathedral with its school or the monastery with its school precede the university in the provision of learning for boys. For girls no provision was made. Only in certain convents of nuns were higher studies pursued, though learning might be privately obtained as Heloise obtained it from Abelard. Before the earliest universities of Salerno and Bologna, of Paris, Montpelier and Oxford were established, the sons of St. Benedict kept the sacred flame of learning from extinction. The fame of the abbey of Bec in Normandy drew scholars like Lanfranc and Anselm from northern Italy, as the cathedral school of Chartres, then in the territory of the English king, drew men like John of Salisbury. St. Anselm is the great name in European learning before the arrival of Abelard. Great not only as England's archbishop of Canterbury, resolute in resistance to the absolutism of Norman kings, but greater it may be said for the profound philosophical intellect that directed the minds of men to the knowledge of truth.

Intellectual Renaissance

Vigorously was discussion waged, argument challenging argument in the intellectual renaissance of the twelfth century. After St. Anselm it is Abelard the Breton, with his keenly analytical mind and insistence on logic, whose name is recalled. Abelard drawing all student youth of Paris to his lectures, arguing that nothing was too sacred to be discussed, no truth beyond the reach of argument. This was more than St. Bernard of Clairvaux, the restorer of monastic life, the very voice of Christendom counselling popes and warning evil-doers in high places, could tolerate. Abelard and St. Bernard were at peace before the former died at Cluny, befriended by Peter the venerable, last great abbot of that once glorious community. Peter the Lombard succeeded Abelard as the dominant figure, and in no spirit of controversy compiled the *Book of Sentences,* setting forth in order quotations from Holy Scripture, from the Church Fathers—St. Augustine in particular—and from contemporary writers on the doctrines of the Church. Of course, such a volume could not escape criticism but its author died bishop of Paris, his work accepted as a sound manual of theology, to be superseded only by the immortal *Summa* of St. Thomas Aquinas.

The guild spirit had moved men engaged in the same calling to bind themselves together in the "mystery" of their trade, and thus created the medieval guilds of masons and others employed on the building of cathedrals and parish churches, bringing the university into existence. ("University" it was called, not because all subjects were taught—far from it, but because *all* who could pay the necessary fees to lecturers might be admitted. Knowledge of Latin was essential, since all lectures were delivered in Latin, otherwise students of every land might enter and the wandering scholars travelled immense distances to attend the lectures of men whose fame had penetrated to the uttermost ends of Europe.) When Abelard taught in Paris no university existed. It was open to anyone to announce that he would lecture and invite pupils to come and listen—and pay.

Students and masters organised the university, which was not originally a place, but the guild of masters and students, similar in form to the craft guilds of builders. The doom of the unauthorised and unqualified lecturer was decreed. Bologna, only second in age to Salerno, which in importance it soon eclipsed, was unique in its organisation. It was managed by the students, and professors and lecturers were compelled to give first-class work.

The twelfth-century university had its special qualities. Bologna followed and surpassed Ravenna as the law school of Europe, its concern being chiefly with legal and political questions. Salerno and Montpelier became the universities of the medical profession. Paris was primarily concerned with expounding philosophy and theology, with matters of pure intellect; famous in medieval Europe as a centre for the propagation of ideas, for the tradition of Abelard survived.

Intelligence and clear thinking, these were the things that mattered, and to the University of Paris came the most powerful minds of the Middle Ages. It was to Paris—and Bologna—Pope Innocent III went as a student and his love for these places never failed.

Oxford, if we dismiss all legendary and fabulous stories of it origin, was an offshoot of Paris. About the year 1167, when Innocent was still a child, came an exodus of students from Paris to the town of Oxford, then in the diocese of Lincoln, and there these students remained. So at least stands the verdict of historical research.[1] Certain it is that twelve years later the University of Oxford was strongly established. And from Oxford, England being then under the interdict in the reign of John, went students to settle in Cambridge in the year 1209. The reconciliation of England to the Holy See, when Innocent III was pope, brought a charter of privilege to Oxford from the papal legate, and in 1214 the first chancellor of the university was elected by the masters—elected by the masters, but elected as the representative of the bishop of Lincoln, the acknowledged visitor.

The intellectual and spiritual vitality of the twelfth century, so abundant that it made the period appear to later writers as the golden century of the Middle Ages, reached its fulfilment more than fifty years later, when the Sorbonne was founded in Paris and Albert the Great and his pupil Thomas of Aquin revealed for all time the truth and beauty of Catholic philosophy, while St. Bonaventure and his brother Franciscan, Roger Bacon of Oxford, each in his own way, showed the developments possible for the soul in quest of God, the mind in search of truth.

Did Europe ever again enjoy such an age of pure creative thought, directed to man's cooperation with the Will of God, as

---

[1] Rashdall's *Universities of the Middle Ages*, edited by F.W. Powicke and Emden, 1936, should be consulted.

that middle age of the twelfth and thirteenth centuries? Yet more than once in the violent disorder of the times of Pope Innocent it seemed that all was lost and men despaired. For despite the spiritual and intellectual activity it was also an age of turbulence and much destructive warfare, that twelfth century.

Empire versus Papacy

The claims of pope and emperor were in fact irreconcilable. The seeds of future conflict were sown when Pope Leo crowned the great Charles Christian emperor in St. Peter's, on that memorable Christmas Day, a.d. 800. Yet at the time it seemed a wise and prudent act to bring all western Christendom under one political head, to revive the old empire of the Caesars as a reborn Christian dominion, the Holy Roman Empire. No objection came from Byzantium where emperors sat as successors to Constantine. The citizens of Rome, clamorous and venal, hailed Charles as their Patrician and as chosen by the people, while the pope, as bishop of Rome, sealed the compact by his coronation. But Charles had misgivings, hard to account for. All went well while he lived. Only after his death, when division of his empire brought incompetent rulers, men of no outstanding gifts, zealous neither for the peace of Europe nor the welfare of the Christian Church, did the arrangement break down in a welter of violence and mutual antagonism.

Excellent was the ideal as it appeared at the beginning, the ideal of the Holy Roman Empire, and for some the vision did not fade from the eyes till its brightness was dimmed in the passing of the Middle Ages, when Europe, it was plain, was no unity but a collection of opposing nations with no common faith and no common policy. Throughout the twelfth century, as in the preceding fifty years, the contest between pope and emperor could not be extinguished but was forever blazing out. Only in agreement as to the true functions of imperial and papal ruler was it possible for peace to be assured. But how could relations be satisfactorily adjusted when spiritual and temporal ruler each claimed a supreme authority the other denied? Admirable as was the conception — the pope to give the law, the moral law and the rule of faith, to the Christian people of Europe, and the emperor to see that the law was duly obeyed — the recurring difficulty was the acknowledgement of who was truly pope and who was truly emperor. Did the pope create the emperor or the emperor appoint the pope? The issue was not between church and state, such as Europe had to face in modern times. The most fiercely anti-papal of medieval emperors never supposed he could decide any point of Christian doctrine or meddle with the Catholic faith of his subjects; the great Hildebrand himself, Pope St. Gregory VII, never claimed political authority over the emperor. It was no mere punctilio the question of supremacy; what it really amounted to was the sovereignty of the Italian peninsula.

The empire was the Holy *Roman* Empire. Therefore the emperor, being king of Rome, would hold the city of the Caesars in subjection. For a while the citizens of Rome might accept the pope whom the emperor nominated, and by whom the emperor was crowned, but to suppose this arrangement permanent was impossible. To Hildebrand with his burning zeal to restore all things in Christ, his resolute unshakable conviction that the pope, being the vicar of St. Peter, must exercise the spiritual power granted to St. Peter, it was intolerable that the papacy should be subordinate to temporal rule of princes. "The pope was the master of emperors" declared St. Gregory VII, and Alexander III would ask "from whom does the emperor hold the empire if not from the pope?" Yet, throughout the twelfth and thirteenth centuries, emperors would not stomach this exaltation of the papacy. In the face of popes no longer submissive to imperial policy they would create their own popes, creatures unwilling to offend imperial authority, whom history knows as anti-popes. (We recognise the character as it crops up at every recurring crisis and time of trouble: the prelate who for the sake of peace will yield to Caesar the things that are not Caesar's.) The pope in the last resort could pronounce the emperor excommunicate and under this terrible sentence an emperor would come as a penitent to Canossa to pray for the ban to be lifted. But the imperial armies could also drive the pope from Rome and leave him fugitive to die in exile. In the violent collision of opposing wills, an absolutism of imperial rule confronted by spiritual authority that acknowledged no earthly lord, the ideal of a Christendom governed in things temporal by a supreme overlord—the emperor—and in things spiritual by the supreme pontiff, successor of St. Peter and a vicar of Christ, was obliterated. The struggle for political supremacy in Italy remained. In latter days the Holy Roman Empire would crumble and pass away as all human institutions pass and as all political human devices for the government of man by his fellows fall into decay. Fiercely the medieval Hohenstaufen emperors withstood the papacy, and the Hohenstaufens for all their greatness, dwindled and became extinct. The Habsburgs clung to the remnants of the Holy Roman Empire and the Habsburgs are gone. The papacy remains. From the Vatican the vicar of Christ still proclaims the Gospel message to the whole world, still speaks with the spiritual authority of St. Peter, and above the clash of arms and the challenging cries of temporal Caesars his voice is heard. But there was small peace for medieval popes when the emperor was forever urging claims that must be refused. The empire, for one thing, was not Europe and never from the death of Charlemagne had been Europe. The Frankish kingdom of the West, medieval France, was outside the empire, and so were the kingdoms of England and Scotland; as Ireland also was. The

Holy Roman Empire was in fact a Teutonic or Germanic empire.

What is called the feudal system sharpened the differences of pope and empire and made the scheme of a united Christendom, with its spiritual head and imperial overlord labouring in harmony for the welfare of Christendom, unworkable.

Problems of Feudalism

The feudal order that grouped men under a common overlord and bound them to his service, not by any means an unreasonable conception of society at an early stage of expanding Teutonic civilisation, had by the twelfth century become established as a system based on land tenure and military obligation. It varied in detail in different parts of Europe and its observance was never uniform. Medieval law recognised the king as supreme landlord, and his barons were supposed to hold their estates as underlords of the crown and to render military support to their lawful sovereign in return. The baron also had his vassals, freemen and smaller landowners bound to serve their lord in battle on the call to arms. Lower still in this scale were the peasantry; for the most part serfs but not landless; holding and cultivating in common the strips of village land that were their portion; compelled, too, to cultivate the lands of their overlords. It was a system that promised protection from above in return for service from below. The masterless man was an outlaw; for his safe protection no one was responsible.

Of course, the protectorate that issued from king or baron was often unjust, often sheerly oppressive to vassals and serfs. On the other hand, vassals and serfs were often far from submissive, and in asserting independence against intolerable misrule broke into rebellion. As for the barons, over and over again they were in revolt, their vassals with them, against the kings from whom they nominally held their lands.

It was not complete, this feudal system, for the cities and towns with growing trade and increasing industry were impatient of rule from without. Self-government through guilds and civic municipal councils appeared the better way to townsmen. Kings needing money not unwillingly granted charters to citizens prepared to pay for the privilege of civic liberty. The town also became a city of refuge for fugitive serfs, for whom freedom was assured on proof of residence — the period of time varied — within its walls. In Italy the feudal system never had the authority it possessed in Teutonic, Frankish, and English dominions. The tradition of Rome was quite other than feudal. Lombard cities, trading centres like Genoa and Venice, busy centres of industry like Florence, recurrently resisted outside rule.

To the Catholic Church and its discipline, feudalism presented grave problems. It presented in especial many problems to the papacy. Were the bishops, and more particularly metropolitan archbishops (these latter often rulers of vast dominions), primarily Caesar's men or overseers of the Church of God? Kings and emperors nominated them, kings and emperors invested them with the badge of office. It was for the pope to accept royal and imperial nominees and confer the pallium. This for the popes of the reformed twelfth-century papacy was an altogether unsatisfactory state of things. The whole investiture quarrel concerned this investing of archbishops with ring and crozier by the crown, since it witnessed to a temporal authority conferring office and claiming in return feudal overlordship. Archbishops, being in fact owners of immense estates, were regarded by kings and emperors as petty sovereigns holding their lands on a feudal tenure that bound them to serve the crown. The system wrought appalling injury in the kingdom of Christ. The best of kings and emperors — and the worst — might choose a priest of holiness and wisdom for his metropolitan archbishop, as William Rufus, an inveterate enemy of things of good repute, chose St. Anselm for Canterbury. But naturally it rarely happened that an episcopate so chosen could be persuaded to give allegiance to the pope when the crown ordered otherwise, king and emperor being near at hand and the pope far away. Inevitably such an episcopate would not be composed of clerics of conspicuous piety.

Then, too, the sin of simony was rampant. Popes denounced it, St. Bernard preached against it; the sin was not uprooted. How could it be uprooted when emperors and kings expected financial profit from the appointments made to bishoprics, when clergy, nominated to the episcopate, must needs reckon how much they must pay on being invested with the temporalities of office? Flagrant cases of selling archbishoprics to the highest bidder were no doubt exceptional; they were not unknown. The wonder is that the episcopate contained as many men as it did in that twelfth century who, despite the unworthy means employed to achieve the mitre, were of upright personal life. But simony was the curse of Christendom and the feudal system fostered it. Germanic archbishops, when a divided loyalty faced them, gave allegiance to the emperor from whom they had bought their metropolitan sees and thwarted the pope to whom they owed but spiritual obedience. The schisms, set up by the emperors with their antipopes, would have been impossible but for the bishops who, with no show of reluctance, supported the imperial anti-papal policy and elected and crowned the imperial anti-popes.

Feudalism also increased the difficulty of dispossessing parochial clergy who had taken wives and concubines. The rural benefice was a feudal tenure, created by the lord of the manor or other overlord to whom may have been granted, in acknowledgement of his gift to the Church, the right of appointing the parish priest. (But customs varied and no universal rule can be laid down concerning the origin and patronage of the ecclesiastical parish as a unit.) Since the feudal tenure was hereditary, the son inherited the lands and obligations of his father. Hence it came about as a matter of course, whatever the rule as to the celibacy of the clergy might be, that to son of a parish priest would fall the benefice of his father. To the scandal of a priest living in unlawful wedlock—the scandal was not so great when it is remembered that the secular priest in twelfth-century agricultural Europe was commonly as poor as the peasantry to whom he ministered and but little better educated—was added the scandal of a son without vocation to the priesthood ordained to the care of souls, just because his father had been parish priest before him. Only by drastic legislation could this grave abuse be stopped and it took a long time to get the ancient rule of clerical celibacy enforced.

It was not enough for popes to contend with these evils of simony and unchastity within the Church, Christendom was threatened from without by the growing power of Islam and by the steady permeation of the anti-Christian heresy of the Catharists.

The Crusades

The sole purpose of the first crusade was to restore to pilgrims the right to worship at the Holy Sepulchre in Jerusalem, to visit in veneration the sacred places in Palestine which our Lord had consecrated by His presence. This right had long been respected by the Arabs who had conquered Palestine. Themselves earnest Mohammedans, they acknowledged the piety of the Christian pilgrimage, and freely allowed a church and hospital to be built in Jerusalem. The coming of the Seljuk Turks from the regions of the Caucasus, in the eleventh century, destroyed the peaceable arrangement. For these fierce warriors the religion of Islam was the religion of the sword, and in their conquest of Palestine, Christian pilgrims were put to death and all Christian pilgrimages, except on exorbitant payment, utterly forbidden. When the Greek emperor at Constantinople, too weak to withstand the onslaught that threatened his own dominions, appealed to Rome for assistance, Pope Urban II called upon Christendom to rescue the holy places from the tyranny of the Turks—who would have destroyed every vestige of Christianity but for the sums they exacted from pilgrims who persisted in visiting Jerusalem. The response was immediate, ill-organised, and undisciplined. Multitudes took the cross, that is, wore the badge of the cross, and set out across Europe on the holy war, to be destroyed for the most part before they reached Constantinople. The real crusading armies followed, led by knights with their feudal retainers, French and Norman in the main. They passed over into Asia from Constantinople and finally fulfilled their mission—the deliverance of Jerusalem. The holy city became a Latin kingdom, with feudal principalities that covered all Palestine. Two military orders, the Knights Templar and the Hospitallers of St. John, were created for enlistment of Christian men prepared to devote their lives to the protection of the Holy Land against the forces of Islam.

So the position was at the beginning of the twelfth century, and for more than sixty years the Latin kingdom of Jerusalem endured. But it was always in danger from the Mohammedan power in Egypt and in Arabia. It was in danger, too, from Greek emperors at Constantinople, who soon regarded with misgivings this stronghold of Catholic Christendom, these Latin kingdoms set up on the borders of the eastern empire. No less was it in danger from recurring jealousies and rival policies of the Catholic princes and commanders of the military orders. In 1147 the first blow fell when the Christian principality of

Edessa was conquered by the emir of Mosul. The news, when it reached Europe, brought distress to many and the conscience of Christendom was disturbed. The call for a second crusade, preached by St. Bernard, sent eastward immense armies led by the Emperor Conrad and the king of France. The Greek emperor, more alarmed at the possible triumph of the Catholics than at the loss of Palestine, frustrated the plan of campaign and his lieutenants betrayed the crusaders to the Turks. The second crusade ended in total, utter failure.

Forty years later the kingdom of Jerusalem fell before the might of the youthful sultan of Egypt, one Salah-Eddin, whom history remembers as Saladin. With dismay and horror it was told in Rome that the infidels once more held in their keeping the sacred places. The third crusade, organised to regain Jerusalem, brought into the field the great Emperor Frederick—Barbarossa—Philip Augustus, king of France, and Richard of the Lion-heart, king of England. Want of unity delayed the progress of the armies, but eventually Acre was captured.

Then with the emperor dead—accidentally drowned—and with Philip, tired of the whole enterprise and gone back to France, England's Richard was left, before he also returned home, to make a treaty with Saladin granting all Christian people of the west full liberty to make pilgrimages to Jerusalem, with exemption from the taxes imposed by former Saracen rulers. For this liberty, and this alone, the first crusade had been proclaimed by Pope Urban. But at the end of the eleventh century it seemed to Pope Innocent III a monstrous wrong that Jerusalem should remain in the possession of the followers of Mohammed—Jerusalem that had been brought into the Catholic unity and made into a Latin kingdom by Christian knights. A fourth crusade was organised.

By this time crusading had become a profitable business to army contractors, to financial speculators, and to the mercantile republic of Venice. It was of little interest to these Christian traders and money lords who ruled in Jerusalem. The crusading forces embarked at Venice and disembarked at Constantinople. There they stopped till in the end Constantinople passed from the rule of the eastern emperor to the sovereignty of Count Baldwin of Flanders, and a Latin, Catholic empire was set up that lasted for nearly sixty years.

The vision of the Holy Land delivered from the rule of Islam was never lost to the eyes of medieval Christendom. It haunted the souls of saints and the minds of lusty warriors. To go on crusades, to "take the cross," was the dream of kings and knights, it was an act of penance that brought sure pardon of sins. The time would come when Christendom would find the armies of the sultan no longer on the defensive but in full invasion of Europe. The crusades of the twelfth century mark an early stage in the struggle of cross versus crescent.

Once it was realised that Islam was the common enemy—whether in Palestine, in Africa, or in Spain—the privileges of a crusader were promised to all taking part in the long protracted "holy war" against the Moors in Spain. The next step was the recognition that others than Mohammedans were bent on destroying the faith of Christendom; that between Catharists (commonly called Albigenses because the city of Albi in Toulouse was their stronghold) and Catholics there could be neither peace nor compromise. And the Catharists were spreading and multiplying, gaining converts in high places, undermining the religion of thousands, preaching hatred of all things Christian. When it came to war, for the issue was clearly one of life or death, it became a crusade, the holy war in southeast France, against the Albigenses.

Pope Innocent III grew up in the era of the crusades. They belonged to the twelfth century, the crusades, as markedly as the rise of the university, of the feudal system that brought armies into the field. Men became accustomed to all the foulness of war, the sack of cities—murder and lust let loose on noncombatants, war with all its horrors as ferocious in the twelfth as in the twentieth century. War against heresy, when success of heresy meant ruin to the Christian civilisation, was regarded as a holy war, and its ferocities were an inevitable accompaniment of war.

Witness of Sanctity

The last word on that medieval age, that "golden age" of Europe, that century of crusades and Albigenses, is not with the feudal warriors nor with the heretics, it is with the scholars and the saints.

The witness of the saints in the medieval Europe of Pope Innocent is permanent, while Abelard, Hugh of the abbey of St. Victor, Peter Lombard—these men belong to the history of intellectual development. The growth and acceptance of canon law is associated with the names of Gratian, monk of Camaldoli, and Master Rowland, future Pope Alexander III, professors at Bologna. St. Bruno of Cologne, dying at the beginning of the twelfth century, left in the solitudes of Chartreuse the nucleus of the order known as Carthusians. Teutonic St. Norbert, leaving the Rhineland for France, founded at Prémontrè the new order of canons regular to combine the monastic life with parochial and missionary activities. Above all St. Bernard, embracing the order of reformed Benedictine monks founded at Citeaux, and therefore called Cistercian, and becoming abbot of Clairvaux, influenced in his own generation the conscience of Christendom and would continue his influence even to our own days.

St. Bernard's sheer evangelicalism, with its passionate appeal to the heart and the emotions, its call to the love of God and one's neighbour; his insistence on the spiritual foundation of faith, on what we call personal religion and personal holiness; the flaming devotion of St. Bernard, these things make irresistible appeal to countless souls in every age. (Of the hymns attributed to St. Bernard it is impossible to declare with certainty the authorship. Not even the familiar *Jesu, dulcis memoria*—"Jesus the very thought of Thee"—so commonly ascribed to St. Bernard can be said assuredly to be his work. Often St. Bernard's prose reached the high level of poetry, but his genius did not include the writing of metrical verse. Two hymns, one in honour of St. Victor the other in honour of St. Malachy, are admittedly St. Bernard's composition.[2]

Encouraged by his friend St. Bernard, St. Malachy brought Cistercian monks to Ireland for the furtherance of religion and the renewal of religious life. St. Lawrence O'Toole, last canonised saint of Ireland, preached justice to his own people and to an English king. St. Thomas, martyred archbishop of Canterbury, and St. Hugh the Carthusian bishop of Lincoln, both of that century, are forever freshly remembered.

Before the twelfth century closed, St. Dominic and St. Francis reached manhood and the coming of the friars was foreshadowed.

To this Europe of surging movement Pope Innocent III was called to pronounce once more the judgements of God. His high task it was to summon before the tribunal of God, without respect of persons, kings, emperors, prelates who violated the moral law; to adjudicate patiently in the final court of appeal on the claims of suitors from every Christian land; to build up and cast down; to deal with rebellious citizens in Rome and to resist imperial encroachments from beyond the Alps; to restrain the violence of princes and place a limit to the armies of Islam; to uproot the spreading heresy that would strangle the Christian civilisation of Europe. To all this work was Innocent III called by God. Upon him was the care of all the churches. Social and

---

[2] See *Saint Bernard of Clairvaux* by Watkin Williams, 1935.

political problems of feudalism pressed for answer. Neither the ignorance of the unwise nor the malice of enemies would stay him from doing justice. Chosen to be bishop of Rome, Lothario Conti, fully conscious that elected God's chief minister on earth he was the Vicar of Christ, accepted the responsibility in fearless humility. For eighteen years, as Innocent III, he fulfilled his priesthood and proved his statesmanship; summoning from all Christendom the bishops and prelates to the historic Lateran Council of 1215 for the reforming of discipline and the amendment of Christian life. It has been written by a distinguished British historian: "Innocent III represents the culmination of the papal ideal of the Middle Ages and represents it worthily and adequately."[3]

---

[3] T.F. Tout, *The Empire and the Papacy*, 1894.

CHAPTER II

Lothario Conti

YOUTH AND STUDENT YEARS—PARIS—LAW STUDIES AT BOLOGNA—FALSE DECRETALS—CANON LAW AND CHRISTIAN MARRIAGE—CARDINAL DEACON—THREE TREATISES—POPE INNOCENT III.

*L*OTHARIO, the future Pope Innocent III, belonged to one of the old Roman families, the Conti, counts of Segni in the Campagna. They came originally from Germany, the Conti, like many of the Roman families that had followed the train of the emperors, and were long settled in Latium. Lothario's mother was of the Scotti, with whom, and with the Conti, the Orsini, another distinguished Roman family, enjoyed a perennial feud. The private wars of these Roman families—each family had its hosts of retainers and fighting men—were the curse of medieval Rome. The citizens, ready enough at any time to break out in riot, found ample encouragement and opportunity for the liveliest disorder when, for instance, the Orsini summoned their clan to battle. At elections of popes rival candidatures were violently supported or denounced, and when the emperor was also at war with the pope, the Roman populace was inclined to back the winning side and take its share of the plunder of the defeated. Long after the Middle Ages were over the uncontrolled pretensions of the "best families" in Rome weakened the papacy and, brought discredit on the Holy See.

But in the year 1161, the Rome of the newly born Lothario was no place for its bishop, and Alexander III, but recently elected, must needs take refuge in France from the overbearing power of the Emperor Frederick I, Frederick of the red beard, Barbarossa, who held all Italy and, believing himself called to walk in the steps of Charlemagne, would have Rome for an imperial city and the pope for an imperial chaplain.

This demand the English pope, Hadrian, had not accepted and Pope Alexander III, the one time Roland Bandinelli, Master Roland of Bologna, learned alike in Sacred Scripture , and the study of canon law, found the demand intolerable and not for a minute to be entertained. Equally intolerable was it to Emperor Frederick that the pope should maintain a spiritual independence over all earthly rulers. Fifty German and Italian bishops assembled at Pavia by the emperor, therefore, decided that a friend of the emperor, Cardinal Octavian, should be pope, and this Octavian duly became Antipope Victor IV. But in England and France, Spain, Hungary, Scotland and Ireland the true pope, Alexander, retained the loyalty of all Catholics, and after seventeen years of schism, with imperial armies marching and countermarching through Italy — to the distress of the country people — Barbarossa admitted defeat, and the pope was left free to call the general council that should declare the law of the Church on matters of gravest importance.

Student Years

Lothario grew to manhood in the years of Pope Alexander's fight for the liberty of the Church. From early studies in Rome he went on to Paris, thence to Bologna.

Three authorities were recognisably in Europe exerting

vital influence over the minds and wills of men: *imperium,* the holy Roman empire; *sacerdotium,* the papacy; *studium,* the university. Between the political supremacy, contended for by the emperor, and the spiritual supremacy that belonged to the Bishop of Rome, no permanent reconciliation seemed possible. Men drawn to the purely intellectual life were inclined to confess their loyalty to things of the mind; to prefer their studies before all else, to embrace learning as the chiefest good. Yet two Englishmen of signally brilliant intelligence, John of Salisbury, in the first half of the twelfth century, and Stephen Langton in the latter, were to play their respective parts in Church and state, confounding the notion that the scholar was impotent in public affairs. Neither in the case of John of Salisbury nor Stephen Langton was learning a hindrance to good statesmanship.

Paris

Lothario was a student at Paris at the same time as Stephen, though the latter was a few years younger. A third young man, Philip Augustus, was also at Paris; with him, as king of France, Lothario would have considerable trouble in time to come. Pope Innocent III, looking back on those years of student life in Paris, saw them as years of happiness. So through the centuries do men and women look back on Alma Mater, for the mists of time mercifully bring forgetfulness of old discomforts and disappointments, and there is only remembrance of how good life was when all the world was young.

Certain it is that the discomforts of student life in twelfth-century Paris were appalling. The stench and squalor that accompanied the noblest of architecture and keenest intellectual interests brought periodical epidemics. Yet this young Roman noble, Lothario, eagerly mastering theology and philosophy in the Paris schools, concerned with acquiring all that may be acquired from professors in lecture rooms, accepted conditions in medieval Paris without expressing distress. Never an ascetic and yet no pamperer of the body, he accepted indifferently what others studying in Paris must needs accept.

Pope Innocent III never forgot Paris and its school of studies that had grown into a university in his lifetime. When they appealed to him, masters and scholars, against the overweening tyranny of the chancellor of the Cathedral of Notre Dame, who because the office of chancellor once carried with it the headship of the theological school, now demanded oaths of obedience and money payments from lecturers and students, Innocent declared such things were unknown in his day and decreed freedom for masters and scholars from the chancellor's mandates, allowing a proctor to represent the students. But, of course, the cathedral authorities were not easily made to yield. They had ruled the cathedral school of studies, and they would continue to rule the university until Innocent's successors set the university free.

What were the theological studies that Lothario pursued so vigorously in the lecture rooms of medieval Paris? The *Book of Sentences,* compiled by Peter the Lombard, that compendium of statements and opinions concerning Christian religion and Catholic faith gathered from the writings of the Fathers, and from St. Augustine in especial, was, it is certain, very thoroughly read, pondered, and absorbed. To the study of the Sacred Scriptures, Old and New Testaments, even more time must have been given, for the sermons, letters, and decrees of Innocent III abound in quotations from the Bible. Allegorical interpretations of passages in Old and New Testaments crop up over and over again in Innocent's writings. The greatest of all European statesmen revealed a mind saturated with the Bible. All his policy is based on the study of the New Testament.

Receiving the traditional interpretation of the texts that made St. Peter the Rock on which the Church was built, assured that the words of the Saviour must mean what they so plainly said, convinced that to the duly elected successor of St. Peter was given the authority of St. Peter and that the gates of hell could not prevail against the Church erected on the rock while time endured, Pope Innocent's strength was nurtured in the fruitful years of adolescent student life in Paris.

Before Lothario left Paris to pursue legal studies at Bologna he crossed to England to kneel at the shrine of St. Thomas in the cathedral at Canterbury. The martyred archbishop, refusing to surrender to Caesar the things that so clearly to him were not Caesar's, had suffered exile and violent death, leaving an example to all Christian priests. The pressure of Caesar on the things of God called for resistance. All Europe saw the present conflict of pope and emperor. The gospel of the New Testament, the tradition of Christendom, the example of St. Thomas of Canterbury, left for Lothario no room for compromise on the issue. On the pope and on no other was laid the very grave responsibility of the chief shepherd of all Christian people throughout the world. Law studies at Bologna confirmed the scriptural and theological case for the pope's supremacy.

Papacy of Alexander III

The Lateran Council of 1179 attended by some three hundred bishops vindicated the papal authority.

It did not concern itself with the doctrine of the Church. Even though the Catholic doctrine of the Eucharist could not be left undefined much longer when Berengarius of Chartres had once raised philosophical doubts and difficulties about the nature of the Real Presence, yet Pope Alexander, an old man now, was more anxious for much needed reform of morals and restoration of law and good order within the Church of God.

To prevent the scandal of a handful of cardinals electing an anti-pope, mere puppet of king or emperor, the Council completed the reform that had made the college of cardinal the electoral body, declaring that without a two third majority of cardinals there could be no pope validly elected. To stop the scandal of illiterate youths ordained to the priesthood and made bishops for family or political reasons, the Council fixed the canonical age of twenty-four for the ordination of priests and thirty for the consecration of bishops. It also decreed that priests must not practise as lawyers in the civil courts nor as surgeons and physicians. In a number of decrees the high money payments exacted by clergy, especially for burials, were expressly forbidden. (But since clergy like laymen must needs live, the demand of high fees for the performance of clerical duties has in some lands never ceased. Of course, the scale of charges varied in the Middle Ages as it does today. Against the cry of the laity at the covetousness of the clergy is the counter-cry of the clergy against the meanness and parsimony of the laity—throughout the ages.)

Turning also to moral questions that troubled Christendom, the Council gave its answers to these.

The tournament was henceforth strictly forbidden. Many a life was lost in these exciting displays of horsemanship, much enmity was aroused. The whole ritual of the jousting field ministered to a pride essentially pagan. The Council therefore declared that henceforth no man killed at a tournament might receive Christian burial. Yet tournaments did not cease for all this papal and conciliar ban. As long as it was the fashion, knights and ladies revelled in the romantic ceremonies of chivalry, and the tournament persisted. (Papal condemnations of the bull-fight in Spain have been similarly disregarded and a spectacle introduced by the Moors still enjoys popularity and retains high patronage.)

The "Truce of God" at this same Council was declared the law of Christendom, and thus the early medieval attempt to curb the violence of warlike princes and check the horrors of war received the sanctions of the Church. Various French bishops had endeavoured locally to enforce the Truce of God, forbidding all fighting on Sundays and festivals, all breaking into churches and assaults on monks and clergy; forbidding further the waging of war against civilians, carrying peasants into slavery, abductions of women, setting private dwelling houses on fire, and laying waste of vineyards. The General Council of Pope Innocent's youth, aware how often the Truce of God was broken, passed a special canon ordering bishops to enforce more vigorously the penalties of excommunication against lords and princes who in their military ambitions despised the Christian law. The voice of the chief pastor of Christendom and its bishops was heard throughout Europe in denunciation of the crimes of war and the entirely unjust miseries brought on noncombatants. It was only very partially heeded.

Other decrees forbad the molesting of pilgrims and of agricultural workers by military commanders, declared all who lent money on usury excommunicate, and ordered that a free school was to be set up by every bishop in his cathedral city.

Law Studies at Bologna

Lothario, pursuing his law studies at Bologna, was eighteen when this General Council assembled and passed decrees for the welfare of Catholic Europe and the guidance of the Christian conscience.

The reputation of Bologna never stood higher than in the years when Lothario was a student. In all Europe in the latter half of the twelfth century, no school of studies drew men in pursuit of legal knowledge as did Bologna. First Gratian, the

Camaldolese monk, and then Master Roland was the recognised master of the law school. At Bologna could be learned the whole body of church law and civil law. The knowledge of law qualified many a clerk for a post in the papal court, the Roman *curia;* archbishops also and bishops needed a priest-lawyer to guard their interests. Then, too, kings needed a lawyer's help to defend and justify their actions. Law, what it was and what its functions were—this the school at Bologna set out teach. Hence to Bologna came the keenest minds in Italy. Unless it was known what really was the law of the Church, the canon law, how was it possible for pope or bishop to give right judgement? Clergy, and in a lesser degree laity, seeking justice, were turning increasingly to the pope as to the final court of appeal, and their demands, claims, and counterclaims had to be justly decided. All Europe must be told what the law decided; on what foundation the legal decision rested. Law, not military prowess, was the final arbiter in a Christian civilisation. This, Pope Alexander III maintained. Lothario, when he came to be chosen pope, would in his turn affirm with no less firmness the supremacy of justice over violence, of law over arms. Emperors, kings, and a multitude of petty sovereigns flouted the law that checked their ambitions and condemned their disorder; yet they hardly dared deny the authority of law even when they flouted it.

Law did exist—that was the point; and Rome was the depository of law and the final court of appeal. The patient toil of Gratian at Bologna had at last, and for many a century to come, made it possible to affirm authoritatively the canon law of the Church. Gratian harmonised and brought into a single code the numerous and often conflicting decrees that were found in earlier collections. He called his book *Concordantia Discordantium Canonum.* The thing had been attempted before; the need of such a text-book was obvious. Gratian's work, known as *Decretum,* superseded all previous collections. It became the recognized text-book and was of utmost value at a time when the papacy was the one final court of appeal for Christian Europe.

False Decretals

As far back as the fifth century, lists of church council decisions and decrees of popes had been compiled; in the ninth century came the historic collections of pseudo-Isidore, with numerous decrees attributed to popes and councils that were in reality composed by the compiler. These, the famous False Decretals, added to genuine decretals by the compiler, were naturally accepted in those uncritical Middle Ages as equally authoritative. Not for many centuries to come would the forgery be proved. No suspicion of forgery discredited the False Decretals of pseudo-Isidore; decretals true and false were included in the eleventh century collections of Bishop Burchard of Worms, of Ivo, bishop of Chartres. What Gratian did was to harmonise, as far as it was possible, the unwieldy mass of material and reconcile apparently contradictory decrees. For what with mistakes of copyists and the inevitable divergencies of manuscript the canon lawyers of Bologna were often hard put to state clearly the precise and exact judgement of the Church.

Of course, our notions of forgery must not mislead us into imputing fraud to the compilers of False Decretals. Forgery in modern times is the deliberate offence of employing falsehood for personal gain. It is false witness. But in the Middle Ages it was not more than attributing to popes and councils what the compiler thought they should have said. (Right down to the time of Doctor Johnson writers—and in especial writers of history and biography—have put into the mouths of orators and public speakers the noble sentiments that were considered appropriate to the occasion. It was done in the case of Martin

Luther.) Again it might happen that an abbey had lost some document, title-deed or what not, that established a privilege or ensured possession. Very well then, the simple course was to forge a copy of the missing parchment. "Forgeries of this kind were made not in order to create a right, but in order to avoid losing a right; documents were so hard to preserve amid the perils of war and the dangers of fire and it is not unlikely that some of the monks remembered documents lost in the fire."[4]

As it happened the False Decretals did really enhance the power of the papacy. The author of the pseudo-Isidoran decretals, for instance, anxious to rescue diocesan bishop from the tyranny of their metropolitan archbishops, made up several decrees that gave bishops freedom from all above them save the pope. The reformed papacy of Gregory VII accepted and acted on this decree, as did his successors, without questioning its authenticity. Thus the False Decretals assisted the process of centralisation. It was not believed they conferred new powers on the pope. They affirmed the antiquity of the pope's supremacy. In no case did the False Decretals confer on the papacy authority in political matters.

To Lothario, the law student at Bologna, the *Decretum* of Gratian expounded by Master Roland, now the reigning pontiff, Alexander III, expressed the very voice of the Church. To all good Catholics in the twelfth century the decrees of councils and popes were of unassailable authority as the law of God, utterance divinely inspired. In the interpretation of the law there would be difference of opinion; more than once the professors of law at Bologna were at variance with the pope on points of canon law. Particularly, was this variance exhibited in decisions relating to the complicated marriage law.

---

[4] See Z. N. Brooke, *English Church and the Papacy* (Cambridge University Press, 1931), on the forgeries of the monks of Christ Church, Canterbury, in the time of Archbishop Lanfranc. Paul Fournier's works must be consulted for the history of the False Decretals.

Canon Law and Christian Marriage

The apparent simplicity of the Christian law of marriage was overlaid with legal niceties and in the unravelling of these delicate entanglements the legal mind had immense scope. Subtle and highly contentious conclusions were propounded by the ingenuity of the canon lawyers. More than once the robust good sense of Alexander III triumphed over legal arguments that brought the marriage law of Christendom into contempt. As pope he sometimes found it necessary to reverse the opinions of Master Roland, professor at Bologna. So his critics said. Responsibility, with the practical experience of human relations that responsibility brings, very commonly compels revision of judgement. Professors at Bologna were free to argue and discuss the exact nature of the law of marriage as long as students would pay to listen to them, to explain the refinements of betrothal and obligations of matrimony without personal reference. The pope, chief shepherd of all Christian people, had before him human beings with immortal souls. Men and women seeking the justice of God at the tribunal in Rome. For such there must be no delay, no ambiguity in the judgement given. The Christian law, the law of the Church, the absolute Catholic law for Christians must be stated promptly and clearly. The pope, God's vicar on earth, he and no other, was the final court of appeal in all matrimonial causes. To his legates the pope could entrust the hearing of such causes in provincial courts, with the pope was the last word.

Lothario, when he became Innocent III, gave the law on marriage, gave it without faltering, without a shadow of compromise when no ground for compromise existed. His legal training left him master of the subject. His very real human sympathies gave him patience to deal with violent, headstrong men, not easily delivered from their unruly wills and affections. For twenty years Pope Innocent and his immediate predecessor

Celestine strove with the French king, Philip Augustus, to compel him to do right to his lawful long-suffering wife Ingeborg, the Dane, "beautiful in face but even more beautiful in soul." Philip of France thought little of the moral law when it clashed with his own desires, but in the end he submitted.

The canon law itself, concerning marriage, was without question in great need of plain exposition. Christian marriage was the voluntary union of two persons, male and female, and it was indissoluble. That was as plainly the Catholic teaching in the twelfth century as it is in the twentieth. Also, this union was a sacred mystery, a sacrament; those who entered upon it received the special blessing of God and grace of God.

But this did not mean, never had meant and never could mean, that any man might lawfully marry any woman. Natural law no less than the Judaic law forbad intercourse that was incestuous. That "a man may not marry his grandmother," as the Anglican table of affinity stoutly declares, is a prohibition that commands universal respect. Who then may marry whom? What constitutes a valid marriage—these were the questions that perplexed the lawyers of Bologna in Lothario's student years. Innocent III followed Pope Alexander in reducing to order the numerous opinions on dispensations, the conflicting opinions of a true marriage and annulment of marriage that was no true marriage; curbed extravagant fancies of the legal mind when at play on the subject. Canon law was in fact in gross confusion throughout Europe in the earlier Middle Ages, and since uncertainty in the marriage law is always hurtful to social life, the pope of Lothario's youth, being himself a great canon lawyer, did an immense service to Christendom by uprooting many difficulties; so that it became possible for ordinary people to understand the nature of a valid Christian marriage and no less the principles of the Christian marriage law when Pope Innocent III reigned in Rome.[5]

Not that all difficulties were got rid of. Cases of annulment have brought perplexity even to our own times. Differences of opinion among exponents of canon law in matrimonial causes are likely to remain as long as the institution of marriage remains. Yet the disputed cases are rare; and being rare attract attention. In the main the work of the great popes of the Middle Ages in this matter of the Christian law of marriage gave the security that men and women embarking on holy matrimony needed. Canon law helped the civilisation of Europe, forwarded the growing change in the relations of men and women, modified barbaric notions of teutonic chiefs, limited the tyranny of Roman custom, adapted and developed the ancient law of Jewry. Once and for all canon law declared, what men and women too often forgot, that Christian marriage signified human equality. It was a hard saying for men of war, the human equality of the sexes in the state of holy matrimony; a hard saying to be repeated by many popes throughout the centuries. A hard saying for kings and emperors that marriage, being a sacrament and indissoluble, only in the spiritual courts could cases of annulment and dispensation be judged.

Europe was Christian in the twelfth century, but the marriage customs varied enormously. Beneath a superficial adherence to the Christian religion and the Catholic faith, Germanic warriors and Roman patricians held with great tenacity their pre-Christian tradition of absolute parental authority and adequate bridal dowry. The medieval papacy, while never allowing that lack of parental consent could invalidate a marriage or that because the promised dowry was not forthcoming the husband could put away his wife, was for centuries engaged in smoothing the roughness of an earlier pagan marriage law, and ameliorating the harsh conditions

---

[5] Consult "The Law of Marriage" in *Church and State in the Middle Ages*, by A.L. Smith, Oxford, 1913.

imposed on matrimony by the sheer weight of masculine rule.

Difficulties of enforcing the marriage laws on recalcitrant heads of families, kings and petty sovereigns, became more acute when the ecclesiastical lawyers of Bologna disputed with the papacy, and among themselves, concerning the degrees of affinity and consanguinity that prohibited a valid marriage, concerning the essential nature of the marriage contract and the means of relief from betrothals enacted in childhood, the question whether a marriage to be valid must be contracted within a church, *in facie ecclesiae,* or at least before a priest — the rule of the Eastern Church, or whether two persons pledging themselves for life to one another were thereby duly married was another matter for discussion. Finally, could a priest vowed to celibacy be permitted to marry? a monk vowed to perpetual chastity be dispensed from that vow?

Divinely guided, the papacy took the reasonable line, the line of common sense throughout this period of argument and counter-argument. The marriage law of Christendom was consolidated for all time. Disregarding the subtleties of Bologna that questioned the validity of a marriage when a bride's dowry was the condition— holy matrimony being a sacrament while a dowry had the nature of a payment, did not the dowry involve purchase, the sin of simony?—the papacy recognised the custom and sanctioned it. Dowry or no dowry, the marriage was good when two persons had willingly contracted to bind themselves for life in holy matrimony.

Parental authority was not lightly to be disregarded; it was the normal and natural authority. Yet it was no true marriage if parental authority forced unwilling bride or bridegroom into matrimony, and young people marrying in defiance of parental disapproval were not to be declared unmarried.

Betrothal, since it directly expressed the willingness of two parties, male and female, to be united in holy matrimony, held by canon lawyers to be a binding obligation to marriage, produced a fine crop of difficult cases. Very young children, often mere infants, for political and dynastic reasons were betrothed; by the time they reached years of discretion the reasons for the alliance no longer existed. Families once seeking closer ties had become fiercely estranged; the betrothal must be annulled. Princes for purposes of military and political strategy looked for a better match for son or daughter; the betrothal must be set aside. Some restraint on the arbitrary wills of princes and nobles was exercised while the papacy remained the court of appeal for all matrimonial causes; some protection existed for young people treated as pawns in the political game while the papacy held them as wards of chancery. Dispensations to annul betrothals were commonly granted by the papacy; because no marriage had been consummated. Prohibited degrees within the extent of blood relationship, and the affinity created by marriage with the blood relationship to bride or bridegroom, provided various conundrums for the canon lawyers to solve and set theorists enlarging arguments.

Marriage was prohibited to the seventh degree, that is, to the seventh cousin, according to the canon lawyers of Bologna, and when such marriages were contracted they could be annulled, being no true marriage. But the pope, in the fullness of his power, could give the dispensation that would make the marriage lawful. The papacy also reduced the occasions for the dispensing power by making marriage lawful for all beyond the fourth degree of relationship.

The question of spiritual relationship between persons seeking to be married also needed answer. That a man might not marry his god-daughter nor a woman her godson was the accepted rule. It was when the canonists would stretch this rule to prevent the son of the godfather marrying the god-daughter, or in the case of a man and woman acting together as god-parents to prevent their children marrying one another that Pope Alexander III on appeal gave his judgement. Spiritual relationship remained an impediment to marriage; it did not invalidate a marriage that had been contracted. The lawyers admitted the power of the pope to dispense at his discretion from strict observance in cases of affinity, consanguinity, and spiritual relationship that conflicted with the prohibited degrees, and to annul marriages that were not truly marriages; to dispense clerics from vows of celibacy, and to permit separation of husband and wife when both wished to leave the world and enter a religious order.

One thing the papacy of Innocent III's time could not do, and no pope for all his fullness of power as Christ's vicar on earth could at any time do: under no circumstances could permission be given to husband or wife sacramentally married and with their marriage consummated to contract a second marriage during the lifetime of the partner in marriage. Grounds of annulment were recognized; separations were permitted, but the latter gave no right to a second marriage. If the papacy could not tamper with the absolute law in marriage and could do no more than simplify and reduce to good order the conflicting theories of the masters at Bologna, it failed in the case of England to persuade the laity in the persons of its chief barons to agree to the legitimisation of children born before legal wedlock. True marriage was the willing consent of two persons, male and female, to take one another in marital union until death. This consent must be followed by the marriage being consummated. Children born before the marriage was blessed by the Church or recognised by the state were the children of a true marriage, according to the church law, since they were legitimised by the subsequent marriage of their parents; this should be legally acknowledged. But the barons of England at the council of Merton would not have it so and held by the older English law. The laity, not the pope nor bishops, insisted that children born out of wedlock could not be legitimised by marriage ceremony, and this disability endured till modern times, but in England only, not in Scotland.

On the other hand, the English anticipated the common rule that marriage must be contracted in the presence of witnesses, in the face of the Church. Quite early in Pope Innocent's reign the council of London required the publication of banns for three weeks before marriage, allowing, of course, when just cause was given, that banns might be omitted and a special dispensation or special licence granted. It is generally true that in the reign of King John the English people were first required to go to church to be properly married.

Cardinal Deacon

The twenty years of Alexander III's exceptionally long reign were over when Lothario, law studies at Bologna finished, returned to Rome. With his mastery of canon law and wide knowledge of the Bible it was inevitable that he should be wanted at the papal court. Pope Gregory VIII, who reigned but a few weeks, ordained him at the age of twenty-six, subdeacon. Lothario was already a canon of St. Peter's. His uncle, Pope Clement III, made him a cardinal. Before he was thirty, Cardinal Lothario was a person of influence at the papal curia, employed and trusted by the four popes who followed Alexander. His name is affixed to numerous papal bulls. To the learning of the schools was added practical experience of the work of the papal court. Cardinal Lothario learnt the business of statesmanship, the art of reconciling wayward men to the rule of law, the science of politics, in the years of service, the years of full employment under popes hard pressed by imperial invasions of Italy. For a while Lothario was relieved by that very old man, Pope Celestine III, of his duties at the papal Chancery; for Celestine was of that Orsini family with whom Lothario's family, the Conti were not on speaking terms; were not indeed on friendly terms at all, though the origins of the quarrel would be as hard to explain as the origin of the Montague-Capulet feud in Shakespeare's *Romeo and Juliet*.

Three Treatises

Freedom from office gave the Cardinal Lothario leisure. He used it to write three treatises. (Many a statesman in later times turns in similar fashion to literature when out of office.)

The first of these little books, *De Contemptu Mundi,* is a medieval essay on the vanity of all earthly things, a discourse on the text of more than one poet of the time. Hugh of the abbey of St. Victor in Paris, Bernard, monk of Morlaix, express in their verses a similar aversion from the world that surrounded them. The familiar lines of Hugh of St. Victor:

> *in hac valle lacrymarum
> nihil dulce, nihil carum
> omnia suspecta sunt,*

which has been freely rendered:

> This grim and gloomy vale of mortal tears
> Nothing that's sweet or lovesome ever rears,
> But from each cranny cold suspicion peers,

reveal the mood of Cardinal Lothario when he wrote *De Contemptu Mundi.* "Vanity of vanities, all is vanity." *The Rhythm of Bernard,* much of it translated into modern hymnals — opening with such lines as: "Brief life is here our portion," "The world is very evil," "For thee, O dear, dear country," "Jerusalem the golden"—strikes the same note. We are, as Christians, strangers and pilgrims with no abiding city in this world. Human life is beset with difficulties, "nothing is absolutely known to men, notwithstanding great and forcible arguments, grounded upon probable reasons"—so runs the English translation of *De Contemptu Mundi* printed in the sixteenth century; its papal authorship unnamed.[6] Married or unmarried, man's life is full of trouble. But for all his awareness of the vanity of human ambitions, the emptiness of this world's glory, Cardinal Lothario was quite certain that not for him was the contemplative life of recluse or philosopher. Sanctity, however, he well knew, was for men of affairs no less than for the cloistered monks, for statesmen no less than for religious. To St. Bernard the contemplative life in religion was the highest choice for man.

Lothario viewed it from a different angle: "While the contemplative life may be the safer, the active is more fruitful; if the former is sweeter, the latter is more profitable." Such was his conclusion. The few short years of freedom from office brought no call to forsake the world for the cloister.

Of the other two pieces of writing, one, on the *Four Kinds of Marriage,* is concerned with (1) the true union of man and woman, (2) the union of Christ and His Church, (3) the union of God with the soul of the just man, (4) the union of the divine and human nature in the Incarnate Word. Biblical quotations and a wealth of symbolism mark this treatise on the *Four Kinds of Marriage.*

The third piece is on the Mass—*De Sacro Altaris Mysterio.* It also abounds in symbolism and Scriptural allusion. Each vestment worn at the altar has an allegorical significance. In every ceremony and rite can be seen a particular sign or symbol. Useful to the historian of the Mass is this treatise, for incidentally it described eucharistic rites and ceremonies in use at Rome in the twelfth century. The symbolical explanations are not of historical value except that they represent the imaginative interpretations greatly in vogue at that period of the Middle Ages.

---

[6] Two English translations were published in the reign of Elizabeth, entitled respectively "The Mirror of Man's life" and "The Drum of Doom".

Pope Innocent III

When at last death came to Celestine III, he was over ninety. The emperor Henry VI, leaving an evil memory as ravager of Italy, ferocious beyond the ferocity of the age, lacking the finer qualities of his father, Frederick Barbarossa, was already dead. Christendom needed a strong pope, delay was to invite chaos. The conclave met[7] on the very day of Celestine's death and burial. One or two names were proposed, only to be withdrawn when it was seen that Lothario was the choice of the great majority. By a unanimous vote the assembled cardinals declared the cardinal deacon elected Bishop of Rome, and gave him the name of Innocent.

It was January 8, 1198, when Lothario Conti, then in his thirty-seventh year, stored with political knowledge, learned in law, at once philosopher, scholar, and theologian, experienced in the ways of man and kindly affectioned, was called to the throne of St. Peter; the throne of Europe as it appeared to many. For Pope Innocent III—small in stature, but according to his contemporaries, of commanding presence and distinguished appearance, the call thus given must be accepted. Natural misgivings, protested reluctance, did not hinder submission to the call. He was the chosen of God, to fulfil the law of God; Vicar of Christ throughout the world and at the same time *servus servorum,* slave of the slaves of God in every land. In the power of God and by the grace of God Pope Innocent would reign over all nations, within the sphere of power which he regarded as assigned to him, since all the nations of Europe to the uttermost ends of the earth belonged to God.

---

[7] Probably in the fortress Septizonium, at the foot of the Palatine Hill, in order to be free from violent demonstrations of Roman citizens. *See the Lives of the Popes,* H.K. Mann, Vol. XI, 1915.

CHAPTER III
Pope Innocent III

CONSECRATION AND FIRST SERMON—JUDGE IN THE SUPREME COURT—CENTRAL EUROPE AND THE NEAR EAST—GERALD OF WALES AND POPE INNOCENT.

SWIFTLY was the cardinal deacon elected to the papacy, swiftly did he assume the full responsibilities of the Vicar of Christ. His ordination to the priesthood was delayed to the ember Saturday six weeks later, his consecration to the episcopate to the Sunday following. There was no delay in grappling with the arrears of work in the papal chancery, arrears that had naturally accumulated under his very aged predecessor. Not yet forty, trained in the practice of the papal court, fully aware of the deplorable state of religion in many parts of Europe, the newly elected pope plunged into work with immense energy. Difficulties in the city of Rome, difficulties in Italy, abuses within the Church, enemies without, problems of statesmanship in the Near East—all these things confronted Innocent III at the outset of his reign and pursued him to his death. Not for a moment—save when serious illness laid him aside—was there hesitation or faltering in the work of his high calling. Hours of recreation the pope enjoyed. The common sense that demands relaxation if health is to be kept was not to be denied. The summer vacation, life in Rome being more intolerable than in most cities in the very hot weather, was a necessity. It did not by any means involve escape from work.

Walter von der Vogelweide, greatest of the South German minnesingers—the twelfth century was the golden age of this minstrelsy as it was of the troubadours—pronounced against Innocent for his youth: "Alas! the pope is far too young, in mercy help thy Christendom." But then Walter von der Vogelweide was the poet and singer of the Hohenstaufen, devoted all his life to the imperial cause and the enemy of a papacy unsubmissive to the German emperor. The strength of Innocent belonged to his comparative youth. He approached untimorously tremendous questions; with vigour impossible in an old man he dealt with each crisis in the affairs of Europe. Yet Walter was never persuaded that the pope could be right. (The English monk of St. Albans, Matthew Paris, is nearly as bitter as Walter in his dislike of the papacy of Innocent III and as frequently untrustworthy in his statements concerning not only Innocent but also concerning his successors. The chronicle of Matthew Paris is the work of a monk avid for news, eagerly interested in public affairs, whose unconcealed likes and dislikes colour his reports.)

Consecration and First Sermon

On the day he was made bishop, Sunday, February 22, 1198, Pope Innocent, sitting on a horse bedecked with scarlet trappings, was escorted with vast magnificence to St. Peter's. All the colour of mediaeval pageantry, all the splendour of the Eternal City can be seen in the procession that set off in the early morning from the Lateran palace to the Vatican on that Sunday in February, with the streets decorated with arches of shrubs and with branches set in the ground. In addition, thurifers beyond number from all the churches and monasteries of Rome were stationed at various points along the route to sweeten the air; a very desirable proceeding in a medieval city that cared little for problems of sanitation.

The pope alone was on horseback. Cardinal bishops and cardinal priests, deacons and subdeacons, abbots and other prelates, admirals of the fleet (these in copes), walked before. Judges and the Roman prefect brought up the rear. So the procession went its appointed way, crossing the Tiber at the bridge of St. Angelo. Within St. Peter's the pope was consecrated bishop according to usage, the usage of centuries; and little changed to-day are the ceremonies that belong to the consecration of a bishop according to the Latin rite.

Then, with High Mass sung and the pope crowned in the presence of the crowd on the steps outside St. Peter's, the procession returned to the Lateran, with many halts for distribution of money flung to the people. More gratuities were bestowed by the pope himself when the Lateran was reached. Clergy and laity alike were remunerated in the customary way for services performed at a papal coronation. Builders of the leafy arches, thurifers, bishops, and nobles all took their fee—probably a small gold coin worth about a dollar in present-day currency. To the Jews of Rome who presented a copy of the Old Testament, in addition to some six pounds of pepper and cinnamon, it was noted that the pope gave an exceptionally large present.

Of course, the Roman citizens were not satisfied with their gratuities but clamored for more.

The sermon of Pope Innocent at his consecration is the memorable item in the day's program. It is the key to his statesmanship in the sixteen years to come.

Slight of stature was the preacher, but he spoke as one having authority, taking for his text the words of Christ recorded in St. Matthew xxiv, 45: "Who thinkest thou is a faithful and wise servant, whom his lord hath appointed over his family, to give them meat in due season?"

For the newly made pope there is but one answer to that question, he, Innocent, is the servant placed by God over God's family, and may he be found "faithful and prudent." From the Bible—the New Testament chiefly but occasionally from the Psalms and Old Testament prophets—the preacher draws his illustrations. The papacy comes from God, for Christ had said: "Thou art Peter and upon this rock I will build my church and the gates of hell shall not prevail against it" (Matt, xvi, 18). Whatever troubles overtake the Apostolic See it cannot be overthrown because of the divine promise. Her Founder is with His Church "all the days even to the consummation of the world" (Matt, xxviii, 20).

The preacher reminds his hearers that as pope he is the servant not the lord of all; that he must exercise his office in the spirit of the first and greatest of the pastors who had preceded him—"not as lording it over the clergy but being made a pattern of the flock from the heart" (I Pet. v, 3). He reminds them, too, that to be set over the household is to be set in a position honourable certainly, but no less certainly a position of grave responsibility. The pope must hold the faith for all, relying on Christ's words to St. Peter: "I have prayed for thee that thy faith fail not, and thou being once converted, strengthen thy brethren." The pope must also be prudent; since he is bound to clear up doubts and difficulties brought before him, give the right answer to questions hard to explain, decide on its merits each case and administer justice, expound the Sacred Scriptures, preach to the people, correct evil-doers, strengthen the weak, confound the heretic in his heresy and confirm Catholics in their faith. God has chosen him to be the faithful and prudent servant, all that is to be done will be done through God. Yet, "who am I that I should sit above kings and occupy a throne of glory? For to me are the words of the prophet spoken, 'Lo! I have this day set thee over nations and kingdoms, to root up and pull down, to waste and to destroy, to build and to plant' (Jer. i, 10). To me also is it said, 'To thee will I give the keys of the kingdom of heaven; whatsover thou shalt bind upon earth it shall be bound also in heaven' (Matt, xvi, 19). You see then who is the servant placed by His Lord over His household—he is the vicar of Jesus Christ, the successor of Peter, the anointed of the Lord God of Pharaoh, one set as an intermediary between God and man, under God yet above man, less than God but greater than man. He is Peter in the fullness of his power, appointed to judge all men but to be judged by none, since as the Apostle has said 'He that judgeth me is the Lord' (I Cor. iv, 4)."

But, he reminds his audience, the man exalted by so sublime a dignity is kept humble remembering he is the servant of all. Thus may his dignity remain humble and his humility sublime. To whom more is given from him more is required; how great account will he have to render to whom the Lord has given the care of all his household! It is not a household of different families, but of one family, so that there may be "one fold and one shepherd" (John x, 16). Over this family is he set that he may give it food in due season.

"Three times did our Lord affirm the primacy of Peter; before His passion, during His passion, and after. Before His passion when He said, 'Thou are Peter' (Matt, xvi, 18); during His passion when He prayed for Peter's faith (Luke xxii, 32); after His passion when He thrice commanded Peter to feed His sheep. In the first passage is the grandeur of the fullness of the power of Peter; in the second the assurance of the constancy of his faith; in the third the duty of feeding his flock."

The flock the pope must feed "by the example of his life, by his teaching, and with the bread of life in the Holy Communion." He did not disdain to quote Juvenal to show the danger to himself if his example is bad:

> Omne animi vitium tanto conspectius in se
> crimen habet, quanto qui peccat major habetur.

> The higher one may climb in pride of place,
> The lower he will sink who falls from grace.

The sermon ends begging them all to pray God that his weak shoulders may support the intolerable burden put upon them—"to the glory of His name, to the salvation of my soul, to the advancement of the whole Catholic Church, and to the profit of the whole Christian people."

Thus Innocent III set forth the creed of the spiritual ruler of medieval Christendom. To this creed he was faithful. On the morals of kings he was ordained to give judgement. The sovereign power of princes was limited to political rule. Pope Innocent, faced in reality by the barbarism and anarchy prevalent in Europe, did not attempt any exact definition of the limits of this sovereign political power. St. Thomas Aquinas would come to define, with many other things, the function of political sovereignty, and its limitations.

The coronation over, Innocent resumed at the Lateran—that ancient palace of the popes, so often rebuilt—the work begun from the day of his election, examining closely papal finances, clerical irregularities, conditions in Rome and throughout Christendom. To the bishops of France and England, to their sovereigns and to the patriarch of Jerusalem, letters of marked cordiality were sent by the pope announcing his accession to the papacy. Legates were appointed to act as judges on the pope's behalf in numerous lands, to deal with appeals to Rome that could be as well settled at home; at less cost to the litigants. With the vigour and energy that made so many contemporary writers emphasise the youthfulness of the pope, and no less with the patience and skill of a mind trained to sift evidence so that on all sides his justice was applauded, Innocent set to work. At the same time, knowing Rome too intimately to neglect supporters, he at once attached his brother Richard to the papacy, subsequently making him count of Sora in Sicily, while his brother John was made cardinal deacon. Nephews, cousins, and other relatives were also provided for. They were all men of ability, loyal men whom Innocent could trust.

Pope Alexander III, bemoaning the evil that came of appointing ill-conditioned relatives to high office in the Church, since bishops were particularly given to making their nephews archdeacons, is reported to have said: "When God deprived bishops of sons the devil gave them nephews." The papacy itself became a scandal by the favouritism displayed in bestowal of benefices on needy nephews, by the enrichment of the pope's near relations at the expense of the Church. Too many bishops were notorious for jobbery, and what would be called in our day "graft," all through the middle and later ages.

It pursues mankind—this desire, on obtaining office, to help friends and relatives at the public expense. There is no period when the cry of corruption has not been raised, hardly a land where the suspicion of jobbery has not found utterance. To distribute patronage without causing offence is beyond human endeavour. The easy-going man thinks first of friends and family, the astute man of gaining supporters from his enemies.[8] The great statesman is concerned with what is best for the whole community. Therefore a really great statesman is not concerned with what people may say. "They say?—let them say!" If the best man for a particular post is a relative let him be appointed, was Innocent's rule. While no man should be appointed merely on the ground of relationship, neither should the capable man be rejected for fear of what critics may say because he happened to be related to the head of the state. Innocent, needing capable, and trustworthy men around him, found them among his relatives and was not disappointed.

---

[8] It was said of a British Prime Minister that on taking office his motto for the distribution of patronage was "forgive and forget"; forgive your political enemies and forget your friends.

Judge in the supreme court

To cope with accumulations of work on the judicial side, the clearing up of unsettled lawsuits, to deal with the causes brought in increasing number to the papal court, Innocent returned to an earlier custom at the Vatican and sat in public consistory three times a week. The lesser cases would be handed over to the pope's deputies, appeals more serious he dealt with personally. In the lower cases the suitor, dissatisfied with the decision of the deputy judge, could always appeal to the pope.

To his contemporaries the speed of Innocent in sifting evidence and in summing up was a thing of wonder. Lawyers thronged the pope's court just to hear him summing up. Some declared they learnt more from the pope—in especial when he pronounced judgement and gave the reasons for his judgement— than they learnt in the law schools of Bologna. The cleverest advocates were made uneasy when Innocent questioned their arguments. In a case that dragged on for four years, so that the issue was quite obscured, Innocent discerned the true issue, explained quite lucidly what the judgement must be, and so disposed of it. Assurance of justice was responsible for the increase of business in the papal court.

But it was a hard task to cleanse that court and the provincial courts of corruption; hard at the end of the twelfth century to make bishops and the great ones of the earth understand that money could not buy a verdict in the court of Christ's vicar; hard to make a wealthy corporation realise that a poor man should not be defrauded of justice for his poverty; hard, too, to get the officials of the papal court to cease from taking presents from suitors. A positive decree forbidding all officers of the court to exact fees from clients except the fees allowed in connection with the registration of papal bulls, and fixing the amount of these fees, was published by Innocent at the outset of his reign. At the same time, in order that justice might be free to all and the poor have access to the advocates, Innocent got rid of the numerous porters and doorkeepers, whose chief occupation was to secure a personal "tip" or gratuity from persons seeking the help of an advocate. Innocent himself refused all gifts from suitors at the papal court—to the confusion and dismay of some who hoped definitely to please the judge, and persuade him to look favourably on their cause.

To the bishops and clergy generally of Lombardy went a special letter from the pope, directly charging them no more to sell justice for money.

To the money-changers and jewellers, enjoying a brisk trade within the precincts of the Lateran palace, making quite exorbitant profits from visitors, Innocent also turned his attention. They must go elsewhere these traffikers, the pope decided. It might be impossible to stop the cleverer people from taking advantage of the simple, the sharp and cunning money-changers from drawing ill-gotten gains out of the ignorance and credulity of their customers; the ruthless in business matters is likely in every age to get the better of his more scrupulous neighbour. All that the pope could do was to rid the papal palace of the scandal.

The reorganisation of the papal chancery under Innocent III meant a vital reform in the administration of justice; it also meant more and more appeals to the papal court. Many of Innocent's judgements are recorded and the procedure of the Roman Curia can be studied. In spite of Innocent's swiftness in arriving at decisions and delivering judgements, the delays were enormous when clients had the means to prolong the litigation and the desire to postpone a settlement. By adjournments, by perjury, by suppression of evidence and by intimidation of witnesses the fatal day could be put off, and in the process the opposite side worn out. The guilty managed sometimes to escape—even under Innocent III at the end of the twelfth century—the guiltless were sometimes ruined. Such things have been known to happen as late as the twentieth century, in every civilised land.

The measure of justice in the average case is the vital test. The recorded judgements of Innocent reveal both the mind of the judge and the variety of cases brought before him.

In his capacity of supreme judge of Christendom, Innocent gave the law on all matrimonial and ecclesiastical appeals. In cases of marriage contracted in good faith but in violation of canon law the marriage must stand, the pope decreed, unless a very grave reason demand that it be dissolved; quoting precedents in support of his decision.

The cathedral chapter of Lincoln asked if contrary to the law they might elect a bastard to a bishopric? Innocent replied that a dispensation might certainly be granted if the man in question was of proved ability with good record of service. But the electors must be in agreement. Circumstances require exceptions to be made.

A monk in Geneva, skilled in surgery, called in to operate on a woman for goitre, had ordered the patient to stay in bed after the operation. Disobeying this injunction the woman went to work and died. But the monk was a priest, and since unwittingly he had committed homicide, was he to be allowed henceforth to perform the functions of a priest? Yes, Innocent said. For, though being a religious, he was at fault in practising surgery, still he had performed the operation out of love for his kind and not for money and was known as a highly qualified surgeon. Therefore let the monk do his penance and then say Mass as before.

Such were a few of the judgements given by Innocent in his court at the Lateran.

In face of open contempt of the marriage tie by Christian kings and princes Innocent was unyielding. There could be no shadow of compromise where the moral law stood plainly revealed to all Christian men and women. Patient he must needs be, God's vicar on earth, for he knew the nature of the unruly children committed to his charge; knew and understood the pride and obstinacy of princes, the power and passion of their ill-governed wills and affections. Reluctant was Innocent to utter the dread sentence of excommunication that placed the law-breaker outside the Christian community. Only when all remonstrance failed was the ban of the Church Catholic to be pronounced against an offender, releasing subjects from obedience to their prince, annulling the authority of governance, leaving the excommunicated an outcast from the fellowship of Christ's kingdom.

The trouble with the French king, Philip Augustus, began when Celestine was pope, and that old, old man, himself much harassed by Emperor Henry VI, after a few attempts to bring Philip to a better mind, left Philip's unhappy queen to her fate. It was not for nothing that Philip II was named Augustus. He had the imperial mind, playing with the notion of descent from Charlemagne, owning no feudal superior in Europe. In his long reign (1180-1123) France from a medley of provinces found the beginnings of a nation.

It was not enough for Philip Augustus to bring the people of France under a central government, in his matrimonial adventures he would be the law and give the law. King of the French, he would marry whom he would and put away whom he would; no pope of Rome should say him nay. But this was not the point of view of Innocent.

Philip's first wife, Isabella of Hainault, died in 1190 and there were those who said the king had talked of getting a divorce from her. Back from the crusades, Philip thought to strengthen his position in Europe by marriage with Ingeborg, sister of Canute VI of Denmark. Of the Danish princess all her contemporaries speak well. Youthful, fair, sweet to look upon, and of noble character is she described; but to Philip on the marriage day, 1193, came a revulsion from his bride that was never eradicated. He said he had been bewitched by sorcery and that the marriage must at once be annulled. If no adequate reason could be found for his personal aversion it was enough that they were distantly related. Let the marriage be declared void on the ground of affinity. The French bishops complied with the royal order and declared the marriage void. Then Philip looked round for another wife and finally persuaded Agnes of Meran, daughter of Berthold, duke of Meran and Dalmatia, to accept him. Vainly Ingeborg appealed to Rome—her letters are among the most poignant of all the letters of injured wives—Pope Celestine was silent. To Innocent she wrote of her sorrows. A stranger in a strange land, kept a prisoner, denied common necessities, deprived of all spiritual consolations; surely the pope would do her right? Innocent replied with a warmth of feeling to this long-suffering queen that she should be righted. At the same time he sent urgent messages to Philip, bidding him put away the intruder—Innocent never called Agnes of Meran by any harsher term than "intruder"—and take back Ingeborg, his good and true wife. Which was just what Philip would not do.

Innocent's next step was to send a legate to France to give warning that the whole land would be placed under an interdict if the king continued to disregard all papal admonition. Philip, remaining indifferent to threats of interdict, merely asserting from time to time his old grievance that Ingeborg had bewitched him by sorcery, and that his dislike of her was incurable, the legate at the beginning of the year 1200 declared France to be under interdict. The French bishops, to Philip's surprise and extreme vexation, obeyed the terms of the interdict, seeing to it that churches were closed, save for baptisms and a weekly low Mass, sermons preached in the open air, confessions heard in the church porch, and the dead excluded from Christian burial in the cemeteries. Philip promptly retaliated by seizing church property and generally reducing the clergy to a state of acute discomfort. Soon it was evident to Innocent that the laity and clergy who had done no wrong were being made to suffer under the interdict, while the king who was the offender went unpunished. Excommunication was the alternative to the interdict and to excommunicate Philip was the last thing the pope wanted to do. Innocent knew the abilities of Philip Augustus, knew how much he had done for France, the order he had established, his services to education in Paris. To Philip was due the making of Paris as the capital city of France. A great king, Philip Augustus, in the history of France.

With no mere libertine was he dealing; of that Innocent was fully aware. Yet not even a great king could openly defy the marriage law, flouting the justice and morality of Christendom. While Innocent hesitated to pronounce the terrible sentence that would make the French king an outlaw among his own people, Philip himself capitulated. He simply could not afford to be excommunicated. In the autumn of that year of interdict, in the presence of papal legate, French bishops, Ingeborg the queen, and Agnes the "intruder," Philip Augustus solemnly acknowledged Ingeborg as his lawful queen and promised to put Agnes of Meran away. On that the interdict was lifted and the king saved from excommunication. But Philip's repugnance to the queen was as pronounced as ever. As for Agnes of Meran, the intruder, she died in the following year and Philip at once appealed to Rome to have the children Agnes had borne to him declared legitimate. This Innocent agreed should be done—though many disapproved—since though no true marriage it had been contracted in good faith, the true marriage with Ingeborg having been declared void by the French bishops.

The unhappy queen was now in a worse position than ever. Live with her, Philip would not, and no canon law of the

Church compels married people to live unwillingly together. Again Ingeborg wrote piteously to the, pope describing the misery of her state, the hardships of a close confinement that was no better than imprisonment. Innocent did all that could be done to ameliorate her wretchedness and bring her husband to do her right. Against Philip's implacable resentment he was powerless. So the years passed till, at length, in 1213—just twenty years after the marriage—Philip yielded and the long-suffering Ingeborg was restored to her rights as wife and queen. All that Innocent had accomplished was the establishment of the moral law. He had disallowed the invalid divorce, affected the withdrawal of Agnes of Meran, and finally compelled Philip to acknowledge Ingeborg as his true wife. Nor in the years of her isolation had Innocent failed to give comfort and support to this much-wronged woman.

In the Spain of four Christian kingdoms, Aragon, Leon, Castile, and Navarre, Innocent had trouble over the matrimonial irregularities of headstrong rulers. King Alfonso of Leon had contracted an illegal marriage with his near cousin Berengaria of Castile. It was the second time that for political reasons he had totally disregarded prohibition of consanguinity. After the country had lain under an interdict for some years, this marriage was finally annulled. But Innocent allowed the children to be legitimate.

Peter of Aragon who, like Alfonso, acknowledged the feudal supremacy of the pope and held his kingdom as the pope's vassal, tired of his wife, Mary of Montpellier, and sought annulment at Rome. His bravery as a soldier in the wars with the Moors was conspicuous, his dissolute life was notoriously shameless. In fact one of the reasons why Peter asked for a divorce was the looseness of his relations with women and his inability to keep faithful to his wife. Innocent, firmly yet not unkindly, assured Peter that no divorce was possible. The death of Mary in Rome, where she had gone to plead her cause in person at the papal court, set Peter free to pursue his irregularities untrammelled. The marriage law was vindicated, but no pope can curb the lusts of princes, or compel men to continency. Nor could Innocent stop Peter from debasing the coinage to the hurt of his subjects.

Central Europe and the Near East

All Christendom was the pope's parish. The heart and mind of Innocent were moved by the troubles in far-off lands; to no appeal was he indifferent. His statesmanship, directed to the ways of peace, sought reconciliation between warring factions. To Innocent, the success of a peace treaty far outweighed a military triumph. Law won victories that outlasted the achievements of war. Against Moslems, bent on possession of the holy places of Palestine, Innocent would have the princes make war in defense of Christendom. War in Europe between Christian princes was a scandal; entirely hurtful to princes and subjects alike. To make matters worse, throughout the Balkan states, and in Hungary, Poland, and Russia rival chieftains, nominally Christian and Catholic in pursuit of power, forever intrigued in their civil wars now to gain Innocent's moral support, now to win support from the weakened empire of Byzantium, not yet overthrown by the crusaders. Restrain entirely these chieftains and princes from their recurring animosities Innocent could not. Yet he could curb their ferocities by despatch of legates and numerous letters. Aware, too, of the deplorable state of religion in eastern Europe, he endeavoured to recall bishops and clergy to a sense of decency and responsibility. Hungary, inhabited by the westward-driven Magyars, its rulers converted to Christianity but two hundred years before Innocent's accession, and no less the Balkan kingdoms of Bulgaria, Bosnia, and Serbia, were forever causing trouble. The sons of Bela III—lesser men than the great kings of former generations—were at war with one another for the crown of Hungary when Innocent was made pope. At war with one another were Emeric and Andrew, not to be persuaded to go on crusade against the Saracens, seeking rather extension of power at the expense of their neighbours. However, when Emeric got the better of Andrew in the field of battle, Innocent managed to patch up a peace between the brothers and so brought civil war to an end.

In all no less than 125 papal bulls went from Innocent to Hungary, for on Emeric's death, in 1204, and after Andrew's succession to the throne, the welfare of Christendom was still far from the mind of the Hungarian ruler. "King of Hungary, Dalmatia, Croatia" Emeric had styled himself, adding to these countries whole districts of Croatia and Herzegovina, called "Roma." But the welfare of all Christendom was the object of Innocent's statesmanship; the unity of all nations in one fold, under one shepherd. For that he contended, while Emeric of Hungary and Jonitza, emperor of the Bulgarians, were chiefly concerned with their own schemes for the control of Serbia. National aggrandizement by annexation of adjoining lands was the foreign policy of the rulers of Hungary and Bulgaria. Nothing did these men care for western Christendom, and quite without understanding were they of Innocent's ideal of a Europe united and at peace. Hence all the statesmanship of the pope had to be exerted to check their ambitions.

Now by gracious concession, now by stern admonition Pope Innocent held his way. Compromise was inevitable. To know when to compromise on the lesser points in order to achieve success on vital issues, where moral issues are not frustrated, is the gift of the statesmen in all ages. Such compromise— we may call it expediency or opportunism—belongs to the peaceful strategy of politics; the alternative is war with its military strategy.[9] In the politics of medieval Europe Innocent was frankly opportunist. When Stephen II, grand jupan of Serbia—his younger brother, Vulcan, ruling a large part of the country—appealed to Innocent to crown him king, Emeric objected and Innocent for a while accepted the protest, since Serbia had always professed allegiance to Constantinople. Jonitza of Bulgaria, with his own designs for the annexation of Serbia, decided to get Rome on his side. Hitherto the country, as far as religion was concerned, had been nominally under the patriarch of Constantinople. Jonitza now promised complete submission to Innocent if the pope would crown him king. Innocent, always desiring the return of separated brethren to the unity of Christendom, agreed to do so, and though Emeric tried to thwart this move of Jonitza's by arresting the papal legate on his way to Bulgaria, the result was merely a delay. For on Emeric's death, in 1294, Innocent sent both crown and sceptre to Jonitza and a pallium to Basil, the archbishop of Ternoko, making him patriarch of Bulgaria. But this union with the Holy See for the Bulgars, who adopted as a matter of course the faith of their sovereign, was short lived. Plunged into war against the Latin kingdom of Constantinople, they repudiated Rome and lost national independence when the Turks advanced on Europe. But all that was after Innocent's death.

Serbia went the way of Bulgaria. Emeric had expelled Stephen and made Vulcan subordinate jupan to the king of Hungary, but Stephen returned when Emeric was dead and, after making many promises of loyalty to Rome, was crowned, thereby securing papal protection. The independence of Serbia thus guaranteed, its ruler turned back to Constantinople for spiritual authority; to be conquered in due season by the Turks.

---

[9] *Cf.* J.H. Newman in preface to *Lectures on the Turks*, 1853, "Political questions are mainly decided by political expediency and only indirectly and under circumstances fall into the province of theology."

Hungary under King Andrew brought fresh anxieties to Innocent. The country was remote from Rome; access to it hard and difficult. Roads were few and bad, the passage from England and France far easier. The moral and spiritual standard of Hungarian bishops and, consequently, of their flocks was notoriously low. The city of Gran had been given ecclesiastical importance by making it the see of an archbishop, primate of Hungary, in order that a closer connection with the pope might result in reform in clerical life. Innocent, looking to the king for the names of good men for bishops, was considerably perplexed when Andrew proposed Berthold of Bamberg, the brother of his queen, a young man of twenty-five, for the vacant archbishopric of Colocsa. Berthold's years were well below the age limit for bishops according to canon law, but the pope had full power to dispense from that impediment. Of Berthold himself Innocent really knew nothing. Since Andrew gave his brother-in-law an excellent character, the pope agreed to the appointment. All too soon he lived to regret it. For Berthold was both profoundly ignorant and highly contentious, showing himself indifferent to the welfare of his people, but by no means indifferent to the amount of money to be extracted from his archdiocese. With the primate of Gran, Berthold was quickly at variance; by the Hungarian people he was quickly hated. It all ended in a popular uprising against the avaricious and autocratic young prelate and in the tumult that ensued his sister, closely identified with Berthold in all his high-handed ways, was murdered. Berthold made his escape to Germany, carrying with him the treasure he had accumulated. (It was that murdered queen who was the mother of Hungary's St. Elizabeth. As for Berthold, he turns up again after Innocent's death, as patriarch of Aquilea; a prelate not to be denied rich preferment.)

Bosnia, an independent state under Culin its ban, presented another problem to Innocent. It was the home of the Neo-

Manichean heretics called Bogomils, found in Bulgaria as early as the tenth century, and widely spread over Italy and in Provence. They were known in Italy as Patarine, these peculiar people, whose principles conflicted fundamentally with the Christian faith and morals, and in southern France they were called Albigenses. Culin failed to enforce the prescription pronounced by Innocent against the heretics when he brought Bosnia within the spiritual authority of Rome. But the Turks, on their conquest of Bosnia, actually exterminated the Bogomils.

Innocent saw Poland, still further from Rome, but nominally Catholic and never submissive as were the Slavs to the patriarch of Constantinople, ravaged by civil war and plagued with moral disorders. The clergy had mostly taken wives and concubines, the Polish dukes plundered the Church and made its local primate, the archbishop of Gnesen, the special victim of their attacks. His see had only recently been created archbishopric, as Gran had been appointed in Hungary, for the better discipline of the Church in these outposts of Europe. To Duke Ladislaus, the most powerful of these rival and pugnacious Polish chiefs, Innocent wrote as a father to a son, insisting that the robbery of the Church must cease and the archbishop of Gnesen protected. There must be also freedom for the clergy in the election of bishops, married clergy must not be nominated to new benefices, and the clergy themselves must no longer profane the parish churches by the performance of stage plays within the walls of these sacred buildings. The scandal of the clergy acting in these plays was sternly prohibited. The response was not immediate, but in 1210 the Polish dukes collectively agreed by solemn charter to respect the liberties of the Church and the freedom of the clergy.

Armenia, Russia, Georgia—Innocent considered all these lands and their peoples and what could be done for their help.

To Russia, rent by the civil war of its lords, subject to the spiritual overlordship of Constantinople, Innocent sent a letter imploring clergy and laity to return to the obedience of the Holy See. The gesture was ignored, the Russians had never known a close tie with Rome. It was from the Greek emperor of Constantinople and his patriarch they had received the knowledge of the Christianity.

The king of Armenia—Leo II—appealed to Rome directly for help against the Saracens and the archbishop of Mainz crowned him king in the name of pope and emperor. Then, becoming involved in disputes with the knights Templars and after much bitter stickling over rights of landed property in the king's dominion, Leo was alienated from the Holy See. A formal reconciliation, that placed the king of Armenia subject in spiritual matters to the pope and the pope alone, was insubstantial. The Armenians drifted away from the unity of Christendom and wished their church to be independent. Only a minority, enjoying to this day its rites and ceremonies, held faithfully to the authority of the pope.

Georgia, lying between the Black and Caspian seas in the mountainous country of the Caucasus, was the uttermost end of the Christendom of Pope Innocent. Its kings and people, then called Iberians, being outside the Byzantine empire from the time of their conversion to Christianity in the fourth century, stood loyally to the see of Rome. (Catholic they remained till by annexation in the nineteenth century they were added to the dominions of the tzar, and so became part of the empire of all the Russias, and subjects of the Greek church.) To the king of Georgia Innocent appealed, urging support of the crusades. But it was little this mountain folk could do in the war of the cross against the crescent, save fight valiantly to preserve the remnant of their nation from annihilation at the hands of the Turk.

All north Africa was in possession of the Moors. The

historic Church of St. Cyprian and St. Augustine had long been utterly uprooted. Everywhere the creed of Islam alone was established. Tidings of the sorrows of Christian prisoners and captives moved the heart of Innocent to write to the sultan of Morocco, urging an exchange of Mohammedan prisoners held by Christian rulers for Christian prisoners held by the sultan. And to this exchange of prisoners the sultan of Morocco willingly agreed.

To the Greek patriarch of Alexandria Innocent also wrote, inviting him to send representatives to the general council of the Church at the Lateran in 1215. Nor was this letter in vain, for Alexandrian representatives duly attended the council.

Throughout his reign of eighteen years Pope Innocent kept up communications as best he could with far-off places. Beset at home with questions of Roman and Italian governance, grappling abroad with recalcitrant kings and princes, presiding in the papal court as supreme judge in causes ecclesiastical, foreseeing with statesman's eye the threat to all Europe that loomed in Islam, we may yet observe him in a leisure moment as Archdeacon Gerald of Wales once saw him.

Gerald of Wales and Pope Innocent

Archdeacon Gerald, *Giraldus Cambrensis,* industrious writer, not a little vain of his authorship and ancient Welsh-Norman blood, egotistical (contemporaries called him cantankerous), could not be in Rome without recording in pen and ink his impressions of the great Pope Innocent.

Four times did this intrepid old man make the journey to Rome in order that he might be consecrated archbishop of St. David's and declared metropolitan of Wales. The chapter had elected him, but opposition had come from Walter the justiciar, archbishop of Canterbury, who saw in the plan for making a Welsh metropolitan a dangerous infringement of the rights of

Canterbury. The decision was left by the pope to the papal judges delegated to England. (After much litigation, with citing of Gerald to appear before the judge delegates, and exchange of excommunications, Innocent finally quashed both the election of Gerald and of the nominee of Walter, the justiciar.)

Innocent had left the Lateran with a few of his private staff for a favorite spot—the not far distant *Fons Virginum*, a lovely marble fountain of fresh running water, in a meadow—and thither Gerald followed him. The pope would have his entertaining visitor—the archdeacon was good company—sit by him, and, after assuring Gerald that the decision of the Roman Curia would not be affected by personal considerations but solely by the justice of the case, invited him to talk about the amusing slips made by the illiterate archbishop Walter in grammar and in theology. According to Gerald, the pope was highly entertained by what he told him and vastly pleased with a copy of Gerald's book presented by the author.[10] They conversed freely in Latin, on that summer evening, capping stories, enjoying the relaxation of cultivated minds, while the water splashed in the fountain and the stream that fed it went brightly through the meadow. Gerald has it all down in his autobiography; the scene and the manifest pleasure the pope derived from his companion. Nor did the fact that Gerald failed to get what he wanted in Rome provoke the censure that throughout his writings Gerald lavished so plentifully on contemporaries. Gerald of Wales in his full life met everybody of importance and his criticisms tend to be scathing. Pope Innocent he praises; praises whole-heartedly as ruler and steersman of the barque of Peter.

---

[10] This was the *Gemma Ecclesiastica*, "The Jewel," and Innocent kept it under his pillow as a "bed book"—so Gerald says.

THE STATES OF THE CHURCH
IN THE DAYS OF INNOCENT III
REAL POSSESSION
SUZERAINTY
SUZERAINTY EITHER CONTESTED OR DIVIDED
STATES OF THE CHURCH
Ferrara
Bologna
Ravenna
ROMANIA
S. Marino
Urbino
Ancona
MARCH OF ANCONA
Perugia
DUCHY OF SPOLETO
Spoleto
PATRIMONY OF ST. PETER
SABINA
KINGDOM OF THE TWO SICILIES
Rome
CAMPAGNA OF ROME
Naples

CHAPTER IV
City of Rome and States of the Church

> Conflicts Within Rome—anti-papal Forces—innocent's Services to Rome—hospital of the Holy Spirit—states of the Church—kingdom of the Two Sicilies.

INNOCENT was a Roman. A Roman citizen. Son of two of the old Roman families, he knew, as one born and bred in the city would know, the people over whom he was called to rule. A turbulent people, unrestrained by the responsibility of an organised civic life, ready at any time to fly to arms at the call of any of the predominant noble families. Rome with neither the inland trade of the Lombard and Tuscan cities nor the maritime trade of Venice, Genoa and Pisa, had no middle class of merchants and traders. It was without the trade guilds that so vitally affected the civic life of Florence. Certain men were employed as goldsmiths, as workers in marble and mosaic. The papal *curia* had its craftsmen as it had its clerks. The professional beggars far outnumbered the craftsmen and enjoyed an insolent independence. Pride in the city of Rome, in the greatness of its past, was the apology of its inhabitants for the present disorders. The families of the Orsini, Poli, and Frangipanni warred with one another and with other families on the slightest provocation or without any provocation at all. Loyalty to these rival clans depended on money paid to their followers. The people were frankly and notoriously venal. Followers and retainers' could be had on payment.

This was the Rome Pope Innocent was called to rule — a city of factions, of violent contrasts, love of pageantry not found incompatible with zest for homicide; a city whose people were now for recalling republican glories long extinct, now for proclaiming themselves subjects of the emperor, head of the Holy Roman Empire, now for swearing allegiance to their bishop, the pope, and at any time prepared to join in the fray when the Orsini were out to do battle with their enemies.

Conflicts Within Rome

Nominally Rome was governed by a senate, a senate of one, responsible for the civil administration, and by a prefect, the head of the criminal department. Unless both senator and prefect were the pope's ministers, Rome would never be the papal city that Innocent meant it to be. It took him nearly ten years to bring the unruly elements into subjection, to establish law and order in a city strongly addicted to popular tumult, to persuade the Roman citizens that unity and peace were to be preferred to the private warfare of noble families. [Murder and street fighting remained what they were, no matter in whose name the crimes were committed. Murder was none the less murder because the Orsini had summoned their followers to kill and slay. Street fighting was ruinous to the people, its attendant miseries manifest. To what profit was the violence, violence that made life in the city of Rome impossible for law-abiding citizens, breaking Up the paths of peace and darkening the counsels of wisdom? But it took Pope Innocent nearly ten years and much expenditure of money to get these simple truths understood in his native city. And in those ten years he was the statesman of Europe, the spiritual ruler of Christendom.

Gerald of Wales, on one of his visits to Rome, noted the queer situation, observing that while the pope's censure made kings' sceptres tremble it could not move the smallest things in Rome, that "he who bent kingdoms to his nod could not make his ill-kept garden in Rome bear fruit."

On his accession Innocent at once acted firmly. He made Peter of Vico, the prefect, take the oath of fealty to the pope, invested him with a mantle of authority, and required all baronial landowners in the Patrimony of Peter—the Papal territory extending from Radicofani on the boarders of Tuscany to Ceprano and Terracina at the southern end of the Campagna—to take a similar oath of fealty. Under Alexander III and in earlier struggles of pope and emperor, the prefect of Rome had more than once been the imperial delegate. For Innocent there could be no divided authority in Rome; Rome must be one and papal. The single senator he deposed, appointing at the same time a *medianus,* or third party, to nominate a senator in his place. On Pandulf, a stout and loyal supporter of the pope, becoming senator, two ex-senators at once started an agitation in the city against the new regime, denouncing the pope as a destroyer of the liberties of the people. (But their enemies said it was done to get money out of the pope.) The ambitions of the citizens of Viterbo encouraged the activities of the disaffected. For Viterbo, bent on increasing its territory, was besieging the neighbouring town of Viterchiano, and the people of Viterchiano had appealed to Innocent and to the citizens of Rome for help.

The position was delicate, relations complicated. The Romans themselves had a fancy to absorb Viterchiano, and they hated Viterbo because its citizens possessed the great bronze gates of St. Peter's which they had seized when the emperor Barbarossa held Rome more than thirty years before. On the other hand, Viterbo, a vassal city of the pope's, had secured help from the Tuscan League, and the Tuscan league was pro-papal. Innocent did persuade the League to call off its forces, but the chief citizens of Viterbo would not leave off their war. Therefore, Innocent, after vainly sending several embassies to the recalcitrant city, pronounced its citizens excommunicate and called on all good subjects of the pope to join with Rome in bringing Viterbo to obedience. It was but a half-hearted affair, the war now waged against Viterbo, and but for the money supplied by Richard, Innocent's brother, might have gone on indefinitely. Viterbo had its hired soldiery and the senator of Rome, thanks to Richard's financial help, hired a stronger force. Viterbo was defeated in the field and the victorious Romans took many prisoners, whom they shut up in a peculiarly foul dungeon. Innocent at once had the prisoners removed to better quarters, and this done, the next thing was to arrange terms of peace. The negotiations were long drawn out. That was inevitable between people with a zest for bargaining, people never in a hurry to conclude any business; and who were in this case far more zealous not to be overreached by their neighbours than to dwell in unity.

The pope at last affected a settlement that gratified the Romans and left the people of Viterbo content. All prisoners were to be released and the bronze gates of St. Peter's restored to where they belonged. Viterbo also promised to leave off the campaign against Viterchiano, to pull down a fortress that threatened the countryside, and in addition to the oath of obedience to the pope to swear allegiance to the city of Rome. The bulk of people in Rome and Viterbo were glad enough to have peace, but it seemed to the Orsini an excellent opportunity to renew their feud with the pope. First they denounced the peace terms as a settlement favourable to the pope and to no one else; then, when Innocent had retired to Velletri from the September heat of Rome, they fell upon the Scotti, Innocent's family on the maternal side, and drove them out of their dwelling places.

Anti-Papal Forces

This brought Innocent back to Rome with a demand to the Orsini that they should take an oath promising obedience and peaceful conduct in the future. The oath binding them to keep the peace was taken by the Orsini without hesitation. To the senator Pandulf it seemed altogether insufficient. He knew too well the strength of the vendetta that kept these families at strife. He required from both sides the surrender of their towers, demolished one of the Orsini towers, and then ordered the Scotti to remove outside the walls of the city beyond St. Paul's and the Orsini outside the walls beyond St. Peter's. The truce was soon broken on the Scotti meeting one of the opposite clan in the neighbourhood of St. Paul's and promptly murdering him. (The unfortunate victim happened to have married a Scotti.) On hearing of this the Orsini rushed to arms and, crying vengeance, came pouring into the city. Not content with destroying the Scotti towers with the houses adjoining, they proclaimed the pope their enemy, since Innocent was of the Scotti, and took sides with another anti-papal family, the Poli.

With Odo de Polo, the quarrel with the pope and with Count Richard seems to have been entirely a question of money. Odo held his lands as a fief of the Church. They were, in fact, ecclesiastical property granted to the Poli family. The Poli, indulging the common taste of Roman nobility for ostentatious extravagance, had naturally raised money on their lands; the Poli estates were heavily mortgaged. To get out of debt Odo proposed a marriage between his daughter and a son of Count Richard, the latter agreeing to the engagement. It is difficult to make out exactly the nature of the marriage settlement; but it seems that Odo had calculated that he would be free of debt according to the terms agreed upon, and that when he found his estates would pass as the bride's dowry to this prospective son-in-law, he broke off the engagement and denounced Richard as a swindler. In vain both Richard and the pope urged that the matter should be brought before a judicial tribunal, Odo would have no judge to arbitrate, no lawyer to interfere. He appealed to the Roman mob rather than to the law. With an organised gang of followers Odo would burst into the churches of Rome during Mass and shout out that he had been robbed by the pope and the pope's brother Richard. Nor was this enough, for on Easter Monday in the year 1203, when the pope was saying Mass, they brawled in St. Peter's, and they attacked him with derisive and insulting epithets when he went in the customary procession from the Vatican to the Lateran.

What could Innocent do with such an unruly flock? How bring order in the city of Rome with Orsini and Poli defying all decent government.

Anti-papal feeling was excited still further when the Poli publicly announced that they had made over their lands in the city to the people of Rome. Of course, these lands were not theirs to give. They were held as a fief of the pope; or as we should say today, the freehold was the pope's. Innocent made it plain that legally the Poli could not give away lands that belonged to somebody else, and Count Richard was left in possession.

Thereupon the Poli and Orsini found another excuse for violent disorder—the high tower, the highest in Rome, that Richard had built largely, it is said, with money given him by Innocent. (The lower part of this tower was standing as late as the twentieth century at a corner of the Via Cavour.) From this tower the Poli-Orsini forces were strong enough, backed by the mob, to drive Richard, and to hold it against all rivals. On this Innocent left Rome. His power was spiritual not military; he had no army of retainers at his command to put down riot and rebellion.

It was not for the pope, chief shepherd of Christendom,

Christ's vicar on earth, to engage in civil war with these troublesome, unruly children whom he knew so well. So he departed in the early summer of that same year 1203 to Feretino, removing in the autumn to Anagni. Sickness fell upon him — Innocent was never a man of great physical constitution; he lived sparingly, frugally, but his energy and immense hours of work wore him out. For a time his life was despaired of, and while he lay too ill to take any part in public life, matters in Rome went from bad to worse. Between the Poli-Orsini faction, seeking to pack a newly chosen senate with anti-papal members, and the retiring senator Pandulf, consistently faithful to Innocent, all civic authority crumbled; all law and order vanished. Peace and security ceased to exist; neither life nor property was respected. Stable elements in Rome—after all the thieving murderous gangs were but a minority—began to look to the pope for deliverance. Innocent was convalescent when deputations came to Anagni begging him to return and re-establish order in the city. Many deputations arrived all bringing the same petition. In March, when once more his health had come back to him, Innocent arrived in Rome; to be received with tremendous enthusiasm.

Innocent's first act was to appoint a *medianus* who should choose the senator. The *medianus* named by the pope, one John Capocci, who had never been identified with Richard's party, chose for senator a quite incompetent person, and so fresh disorders occurred. A group of self-elected senators denied the pope's right to appoint a senator. With much indignation they demanded restoration of popular rights. Capocci and others began to build towers and prepare for a fight. Pandulf and his party, helped with Conti money, also took up arms to put down the rebellion. They in their turn built towers. Ruins of ancient monuments provided stone.

Once more the city was given over to civil war. Century old baths were fortified, ancient churches turned into fortresses.

The antiquities of the city were nothing to these turbulent people. Rome suffered more than once from the foreign invader, but no enemy from without inflicted such ruin on its past architectural loveliness as did its citizens. Boast they would of the ancient glories of imperial Rome, preserve or reverence tokens of the past they would not. Stone or wood wanted for their continual faction fights was freely taken wherever found. (In centuries to come, by restoration and rebuilding, even worse architectural outrage would be brought.)

For a time Capocci, now backed by another powerful Roman family, the Frangipani, had the better of this street fighting, but Pandulf and the pope's brother-in-law, Peter Anibaldi, were victorious in the end. Once more appeal was made to Innocent to make peace. While the papal party asked for the total annihilation of their enemies the pope sought reconciliation. Innocent proposed an enquiry by four "good men" into the question of the rights of the pope and the citizens concerning the election of the senate. The Capocci party rejected the proposal with scorn: "never had Rome yielded to the Church in any contested matter; always had it relied on force in its conquests, never on law." Capocci's return to civil war ending in his complete defeat, the anti-papalists agreed to the question being submitted to the four "good men," who quickly decided that it belonged to the pope to create the senate and recommended that a senate of fifty-six should be chosen.

Innocent, knowing that with so large a senate it would be difficult in a city like Rome to maintain law and order, advised the choice of a single senator; yet for the sake of peace he allowed the whole number to be appointed. The fifty-six being quite unable to agree as to what was to be done, riot and tumult were resumed. Then once more the law-abiding element appealed to Innocent to name one strong man as senator, and the man named brought back peace and justice to the city. That was in 1205, and for a while the order reestablished endured.

The last outbreak took place in 1208, and Innocent left the city on this fresh renewal of disorder. But now all Rome, save the anarchist minority of an anti-papal senator, wanted him back. The nobles were tired of civil war, Innocent was the one hope of peace. Let the dissident senator resign and the pope appoint who he would of the Roman nobility to the office.

The ten years of trouble, of riot and intermittent warfare, were ended when Innocent was met on his return to Rome by all the pageantry of the city. Nobility and soldiery, gorgeously arrayed, Christians and Jews, every section of the community joined in welcoming Pope Innocent. At last he was lord of the city. Bishop of Rome, caring for his own people, Innocent relieved his improvident, restless, and generally idle populace in a year of famine and protected the very money-lenders, then as now hateful to their debtors.[11] Much, too, he spent on mosaic and marble for the churches in Rome and on the employment of silversmiths for the sacred vessels of the altar. Rome under Innocent had its school of artists, a school that lasted till the city was left desolate when the popes removed their court to Avignon.

Services to Rome—Hospital of the Holy Spirit

The greatest of all Innocent's services to the citizens of

---

[11] The question of usury and a lawful rate of interest was already demanding attention in trading cities in Italy. At Milan, in 1187, it was settled that 15 percent was the legal interest on borrowed money, but this was reduced to 12 percent twenty years later. Certain borrowers in urgent need of money got around the law by agreeing to the sale of their lands and the repurchase at a higher figure. St. Thomas Aquinas dealt with the ethics of money-lending and the right of the money-lender to an interest on his money. Nothing could stop usury when there was money to be borrowed, bankers prepared to lend it. The aphorism of an anonymous fifteenth-century writer expresses the dilemma: "He who practiseth usury goeth to Hell, but he who practiseth it not tendeth to destitution."

Rome was the foundation of the hospital of the Holy Spirit. The old hostel for English pilgrims, the *Schola Anglorum,* had by the end of the twelfth century lost its usefulness. Conditions in Rome were not favourable to pilgrimages. The time had come for the house to be dissolved. On its site, partly with the balance of its funds, partly from his own resources, Innocent erected the hospital that became the first of any size in Europe and for centuries was the largest. The hospital is that of *Santo Spirito,* originally called St. Maria in Saxia. Many times rebuilt, it still stands on the Vatican side of the Tiber by the Vittorio Emanuele bridge, it was not the first hospital to be opened in Europe, the *Santo Spirito.* Brother Guido, with his confraternity of the Holy Spirit for the care of the sick, was at work in Montpellier twenty years before Innocent founded his hospital in Rome. It was in fact to Montpellier Innocent looked. To Brother Guido's confraternity he entrusted the new hospital and from this confraternity it took its name. Inspired by the charity of God, the brethren of the confraternity brought into the hospital all sick persons whom they found in the streets of Rome, sought out all who needed the nursing and medical aid that was impossible to be given in overcrowded and insanitary houses, encouraged friends and relatives to bring all persons suffering from wounds, accidental injuries, and common afflictions to the care of the hospital. Innocent would have the hospital in Rome a centre of healing, where, as at Montpellier, "the hungry might be fed, the naked clothed, the sick supplied with every necessary help and those in greatest need receive the greatest help. Money, of course, was needed. Therefore, from his private purse Innocent contributed to the hospital. He did more than that, for he authorised the confraternity to collect for its support throughout Italy and Sicily and in England and Hungary. Not content with opening this hospital in Rome, Innocent next urged that similar hospitals should be established throughout Europe. He lived to see this done in

Germany.

It has been asserted that Innocent was the founder of the modern city hospital and there is truth in the assertion. He was certainly the pioneer of the general hospital in Europe, for a number of German hospitals trace their foundation to the reign of Pope Innocent. Statesman of Europe that he was, Innocent saw the misery and disease at his own door and from the duty to his neighbour his eyes were never turned away.

STATES OF THE CHURCH

While the citizens of Rome plagued the peace of the city for so many a year, Innocent also had his troubles in the States of the Church, those lands of Italy where the pope was sovereign lord, and the people and their immediate rulers his vassals. Pepin, father of Charlemagne, in his zeal for the welfare of the pope and to secure papal freedom from the warlike kings of Lombardy, created the States of the Church in the middle of the eighth century, when the shadow of Byzantine authority that lingered at Ravenna finally disappeared.[12] That the pope should be politically independent of all earthly kings seemed a plain necessity. Innocent gave his reasons for maintaining an independence often threatened and often annihilate—"where the church of Rome both in temporal and in spiritual matters exercises its full power there the liberty of the Church is best secured." He further insisted that within these territories of the Patrimony of St. Peter, of the Campagna to the south of Rome and the Sabina region, good order must be set up, "since as the Apostolic See proves itself the mother and mistress of all the churches and clergy, so is it discredited and with it all the churches if the Apostolic See cannot keep within its own

---

[12] Legends of a "Donation" by the emperor Constantine to the bishop of Rome are legends. History knows nothing of such a gift. The whole story is a late invention.

Patrimony the local churches from losing their freedom."

At the outset of his reign Innocent announced his sovereignty over all the States of the Church. The current feudal system he fully accepted, not believing it to be of divine institution or a universal and everlasting order, but recognising in feudalism the most serviceable arrangement of the time for the maintainance of law and order in Europe. The alternatives to feudalism were absolute tyranny or anarchy—either condition hurtful to man, harmful to the Christian civilisation. And it was the Christian civilisation that Innocent laboured to build up and preserve. Without the authority of civil law, a general respect for mutual obligations that bind men and women in every community, there was no civilisation; without civilisation no freedom to practise the Christian religion. Feudalism at least offered a framework for civilised and Christian life. Unhappily, at the close of the twelfth-century feudalism for German knights and princes meant nothing but military obedience to the head of the clan, loyalty to king or emperor easily withdrawn or transferred when occasion suggested change of lordship. Of all this Innocent was aware. In Italy the Teutonic element was immensely strong, for the emperors had bestowed vast estates on their followers, and from this element came the challenge to Innocent's overlordship.

Between the feudalism of the Middle Ages and the central government of the pope a fundamental opposition existed; a grave and irreconcilable antagonism. Not that it appeared irreconcilable to Pope Innocent. For him the two systems were not necessarily in antagonism at all. Feudalism with its divisions and subdivisions of the European family, each man bound to serve the ruler immediately above him, had its limits. It belonged to the political and temporal order of human government. The centralisation of the holy Roman Church that reached its full development under Innocent III pertained to the ecclesiastical and spiritual order. The supreme government of the Christian Church was autocracy. The pope, duly and properly chosen by the cardinals in conclave, was Vicar of Christ, God's representative on earth, sovereign lord in things spiritual throughout the world; to be judged by no man. In his hands was the appointment of all bishops—though he might willingly accept the nominations or recommendations to bishoprics made by kings and princes. From the decisions of the Vatican on disputed points of law there was no appeal.

All this high doctrine of papal authority, with the ramifications of ecclesiastical government that sprang from it, making the papal court the centre of an organisation that knew no boundaries but the uttermost ends of the earth, was simple, divinely revealed, truth to Pope Innocent. It was held and fervently believed by many of the holiest and wisest minds of the Middle Ages, doubted and questioned by subtle intellects, flouted by emperors and other sovereign rulers, openly denied by Moors and Saracens—followers of the prophet Mohammed—and by the anti-Christian heretics of southern France. To the Teutonic fighting men, who held their lands as vassals in Italy and elsewhere, it was an incomprehensible idea.

That Pope Innocent, feudal lord of the States of the Church in Italy, was also God's vice-regent, was something hardened men, whose trade was plunder, whose method was murder, could hardly be expected to understand. They, for the most part warrior brigands who had received their lands for services to the imperial Hohenstaufen family, regarding the pope as the traditional enemy of the German emperor, dismissed solemn pronouncements concerning papal absolutism and ecclesiastical centralisation as stuff and nonsense. What did these brigand chiefs in Italy, some of whom lived by sheer highway robbery, extorting money from pilgrims and travellers to Rome, care for papal authority? They cared nothing for the Christian religion; when it suited them, encouraging the missionaries of the

Manichean heresy to invade the Patrimony of St. Peter. What did Markwald of Anweiler, that trusted favourite of the late emperor Henry VI, care for the pope? Markwald, "seneschal of the Empire, duke of Ravenna and Romaniola, marquis of Ancona," described by Innocent as "rich and powerful, clever and bold," a man of "evil memory," defied excommunication and, when driven to submit to the papal overlordship of the March of Ancona, went south to Sicily there to wage war and spread anarchy till his death.

The very size of the States of the Church, stretching down the Adriatic coast east of the Appenines, beyond Ferrara in the north and to the southern end of Ancona, including the duchy of Spoleto and much of Tuscany in middle Italy, in addition to the Campagna and the Patrimony was a cause of the pope's grave responsibility. Over all these territories he must rule as suzerain, rule justly, compelling his vassals—certain of whom openly questioned the papal suzerainty in their particular case—to acknowledge law, cease from violence and pay their dues. Innocent, aware of the distraction of temporal rule—he alluded to it more than once—would not seek to escape responsibility. He could not allow that peaceful, industrious people, living within his dominions, should be left to the mercy of robbers and murderers. It was committed to him, this responsibility in temporal matters; he must needs be faithful to his trust. He must prove in temporals no less than in spirituals the justice of his stewardship, show himself the faithful householder whom the Master had set over His goods. Sovereign of the States of the Church, Innocent would be called, as every earthly sovereign is called, to give an account of his stewardship.

Not all the underlords in the papal states were of the character of Markwald. Three at least swore fealty to Innocent on his accession. Others in the general uprising against the Teutonic barons in Italy, that occurred on the death of the emperor Henry, gladly made their submission to the pope. Innocent himself, to strengthen his rule in the Patrimony, placed certain of his relatives in charge of important key positions. Yet for all his efforts to bring the States of the Church under the obedience of the Apostolic See and under the supremacy of law, it took Innocent ten years to bring the people of the Patrimony to submit. To the very end of his reign the March of Ancona was but indifferently subject to his authority, while the archbishops of Ravenna never surrendered the independence they claimed to exercise as temporal rulers by virtue of earlier papal rescripts.

Trouble also came from cities, as eager to wage private wars one with another as were the noble families of Rome. And in this atmosphere of fratricidal strife and passionate hate it was natural that the Christian religion should be ill- regarded and a door opened to the preachers of anti-Christian heresy, to the Patarines, violently anti-papal. These Manichean missionaries descend upon Viterbo and Orvieto from Florence and Lombardy and, according to a contemporary writer, taught the people that all popes since St. Sylvester (314-335) were in hell, that St. Peter was no better than any good man, and that the whole visible world was created by the devil. To the leaders of a popular agitation, both in Orvieto and Viterbo, seeking complete independence from the overlordship of the pope, this doctrine was fairly congenial, especially the articles that denounced the papacy. Patarines and Catholics were at war in both cities, but the murder of the Catholic *podesta* in Orvieto was the ruin of the Patarine party. The presence of Innocent in Viterbo and the great assembly he held in that city in September, 1207, marked the end of the anti-papal movement and drove the Patarines to flight. Innocent expressed the shame he felt that this heresy of the Manichean Catharists should have existed in the very Patrimony of St. Peter; the Roman Church itself corrupted by heresy. How could he urge the uprooting of heresy elsewhere if within his own household there was taint? Would it not be said to him "Physician heal thyself" (Luke iv, 23) ? or "Cast first the beam out of thy own eye and thou shalt see clearly to take the mote from thy brother's eye" (Luke iv, 42)?

Ten years in all it was before the Catharists ceased from troubling the States of the Church, before civil law and order displaced the anarchy and despotism that alternated so widely in the papal dominions. But in the end the Catharists were driven out and Innocent ruled.

Kingdom of the Two Sicilies

The Norman kingdom of the Two Sicilies—the island of Sicily and all the southern part of Italy including large territories north of Naples—was from his accession the special care of Innocent. Constance, the widowed empress of Henry VI, before her death in the November of Innocent's first year, made over the sovereignty of the kingdom to Innocent and appointed him protector of her young son, Frederick, then but four years old. Innocent accepted the guardianship, and when the boy-king was crowned at Palermo confirmed the coronation. From that time till Frederick married and came of age, the care of his ward and the welfare of this kingdom of the Two Sicilies was a constant anxiety to Innocent. Suzerain and protector of the royal orphan—one more burden was laid on Innocent and it was no light burden. Throughout the kingdom of the Sicilies violence flourished; religion was set at nought; the higher clergy of the emperor's appointment, possessed by ambition, were themselves instruments of disorder.

Innocent, before agreeing to do what the empress asked him, insisted that if the pope was to become guardian of the child-king and suzerain of the kingdom, then the bishops must be of the pope's approval; men no longer chosen by the crown, but freely elected according to canon law by the clergy; also the kingdom must receive papal nuncios. Constance, despite her Norman pride with its tenacity to supreme rule in Church and State, yielded. For her all aims were directed to one expectation—all hopes concentrated on one clear view—her son, the child Frederick, future emperor. Without the protection of the pope, hardly, as she saw it, was this to be accomplished.

By persuasion and strong remonstrance, now with leniency, now with solemn sentence of excommunication, now with compulsion of arms, Innocent laboured in this kingdom of the Two Sicilies as he laboured throughout Italy to reduce anarchy to order, to subdue the violent elements that disrupted the Christian community, to compel obedience to law and bring in peace. From the first he co-operated with Constance, anxious to preserve the heritage of her son. Fully aware were pope and widowed empress that neither security of life nor neighbourly intercourse were possible while on the mainland of Italy and in the island of Sicily the hated Teutonic soldiery plundered the country-side; while such a man as Markwald of Anweiler ruled as petty tyrant in Apuleia, waging wars that were no more than marauding expeditions, openly defying the suzerainty of the pope, as he openly defied all law of God or man; planning at times the invasion of the Romagna; forever at war, with a fierce ambition to be supreme lord of the Sicilies.

On the island of Sicily the chief obstacle to law and order was Walter, bishop of Troia, whom the emperor Henry had made his chancellor. A deadly enmity between bishop Walter and Markwald brought a temporary submission of the chancellor to Pope Innocent. Of no consequence was this submission; all that Walter wanted was to overthrow Markwald, and once satisfied that Markwald no longer threatened his safety, the chancellor-bishop returned to his evil ways. Lands and revenues of the boy-king were wasted by this episcopal chancellor whose duty it was to act as steward of the property.

Cunning enough was bishop Walter when it suited him; not hesitating to make up to Innocent, with flattering promises of loyalty to the Apostolic See, for a while persuading Innocent to withdraw the ban of excommunication. Little is it but a record of greed and the lust of power in the years when Frederick grew from boyhood to youth in his devastated kingdom; Markwald and bishop Walter each seeking the control of the boy-king and the rule of his kingdom, employing Saracens and Greeks of the Sicilies to that end. Diepold, count of Acerra, was Markwald's ablest soldier, but Innocent's trusted representative, Walter of Brienne, with his French knights finally overthrew the Teutonic forces of Markwald and Diepold. The names of these men stand out in the confused annals of the war in the Sicilies. Only on the death of Markwald did the hopes of peace return. Bishop Walter lived to make a fresh submission to the pope, to be freed of excommunication and to be restored to the chancellorship he had so grossly abused. Even then war was not over on the island of Sicily. The seamen of Pisa and Genoa, with Saracens and Greeks, continued the evil work. But on the mainland Innocent came in state to pacify. As he had brought peace within the Patrimony by his assembly at Viterbo so with a great retinue he brought peace at San Germane.

Innocent's policy throughout the stormy troubled years had never weakened. He must be faithful to his guardianship of the boy-king, Frederick, and maintain the suzerainty entrusted to him by the widowed Constance. Markwald and the chancellor, Bishop Walter, each striving for mastery of the kingdom and control of Frederick, had to be frustrated. Innocent fell back on the French troops of Walter of Brienne when spiritual forces were held in contempt. First and last Pope Innocent was a Christian statesman, fully conscious that on occasion force and military strength must be used to defeat the hosts of disorder, the iniquities of unscrupulous power. Innocent lived to see his policy in the Two Sicilies successful, with Frederick declared of age at fourteen and betrothed to Constance, sister of Pedro II, king of Aragon and widow of Emeric, king of Hungary. The match was made by the pope, and the marriage brought many nobles and some 500 knights to Frederick's support.

But the revenues of his kingdom of the Two Sicilies were utterly depleted when Frederick became king and the brigandage in southern Italy and in Sicily was not at an end. Far from it. Brigandage was not to end for many centuries to come. It was too well organized to be suppressed. It was in fact a prosperous industry, soon to become a traditional occupation.

Frederick, emerging from his tutelage, no barbarian—for his guardian had been at pains to provide for the education of his ward—would figure conspicuously in days to come in the conflict of pope versus emperor.

CHAPTER V
Pope Innocent and the Empire

> Imperial Throne Vacant—Rival Emperors—Innocent Supports Otto of Brunswick—Otto Sole Emperor—Hostility in Rome—Otto Excommunicated—Election of Frederick II.

INNOCENT grew to manhood in the years of acute conflict between the papacy and the empire. Years of storm and stress for the people of Italy, years of bitter discomfort for the popes—old, old men, without strength to combat such a ruler as Frederick Barbarossa or his son Henry VI. The latter by his marriage with Constance, heiress of the Norman kingdom of the two Sicilies, had become predominant in Italy. Very precarious was the independence of the pope when the emperor controlled the greater part of middle Italy though his Teutonic feudal tenants, counted Lombardy for the time a vassal state, and reigned in the Sicilies.

Imperial Throne Vacant

For Innocent, on his accession, happily there was a lull in the recurring conflict that politically overshadows the history of medieval Europe. Henry was dead, leaving his son an infant. True, before his death Henry had persuaded the prince electors of Germany to elect his son, but an infant emperor was impossible; and besides, there were many in Germany stubbornly against the hereditary principle that made the empire the perquisite of the Hohenstaufen family.

The Holy Roman Empire then had no emperor when Lothario Conti became Pope Innocent III; a situation that provoked profound misgivings in Germany where the late emperor, hated in Italy for his masterful tyranny, was mourned as a great rule.

The respite was short. Before the end of Innocent's first year of office all the horrors of civil war tormented the Teutonic peoples. Two candidates claimed the imperial throne. Philip of Swabia, the Hohenstaufen, brother of Henry VI, and Otto of Brunswick, son of Henry the Lion of Bavaria—that relentless fighter against the Hohenstaufen emperor, Frederick Barbarossa, and nephew of Richard I of England—young men, both these claimants to the empire; under twenty-five and well spoken of by contemporary writers. Otto, taller and more handsome, the better soldier, but often rash and unfaithful to his word. Philip, a good soldier, too, though of no great bodily strength, with finer qualities of mind and the more generous character. For all the engaging qualities of the rival emperors, the war was waged with horrible ferocity. It was the war of Guelph versus Ghibelline that from Germany would be carried to Italy, there to produce foul crops of murder in the century to come.

Rival Emperors

Otto of Brunswick was Guelph—Welf was the family name — the enemy of the empire represented by the Hohenstaufen. The first and only Guelph to be elected emperor.[13]

---

[13] The British royal family is of Guelph descent, since George I, elector of Hanover, was of the house of Brunswick.

Philip of Swabia was Ghibelline, that is, Waiblingen, so named after a town in Würtemburg. "Waiblingen" was the battle cry of the Hohenstaufen in their earlier wars against the Henry-the-Lion party, while the latter shouted "Welf." The traditional Hohenstaufen policy was anti-papal, the Guelph policy was anti-Hohenstaufen, only in a secondary way pro-papal. When the feud was extended to Italy the northern parts were in the main Ghibelline, the central and southern Guelph. But no clear-cut division can be traced and cities were as often as not fiercely split into the rival factions.

Philip of Swabia was first in the field, hurrying back to Germany from Sicily before the popular rising on Henry's death could overwhelm him. By an immense expenditure of money, spoils of the kingdom of the Sicilies, Philip won sufficient support of the prince-electors to be chosen emperor in the spring of 1198. Otto with money from his uncle, Richard of England, managed to get election by another body of these highly corruptible prince-electors. Later in being chosen emperor, Otto made up for this by getting the archbishop of Cologne to crown him at Aachen (Aix-la-Chapelle) some months before Philip was crowned. By the end of the year both emperors were seeking support and approval from Innocent. It was now for the pope to say who was the true emperor and who the anti-emperor.

No hasty decision came from Innocent. Now as always his desire was the welfare of Christendom, his policy the peace of Europe.[14] With careful consideration he weighed the respective merits of the imperial claimants before pronouncing judgement. But for Philip or Otto there was no waiting; to them the welfare of Christendom was an idle dream, the peace of Europe a vain chimera. The arbitrament of war was for these Teutonic minds the settlement of disputes. The fortune of war at the outset

---

[14] He had the utmost zeal for the extension of the Kingdom of Christ"–Tout, *Empire and Papacy*, 1898.

favoured Philip of Swabia; his supporters, bishops and nobles, wrote to the pope that he was their duly elected emperor and that they would maintain his rights to all the authority exercised by his predecessor, Henry VI.

Innocent would not have his hand forced. Because he so fully recognised the importance of the empire as a factor in the politics of Europe, he felt his responsibility the greater. The power and influence of the emperor for good and for evil being what they were, the imperial crown could not be awarded without grave deliberation. For the empire itself Innocent had the strongest regard. He held it to be a permanent institution, necessary for the security of mankind. A human institution of a usefulness beyond account. The loss of the empire, Innocent wrote while the war of Philip and Otto wasted middle Europe, would be a disaster to the Christian Church. It was the pope who had transferred the empire from the Greeks (when Charlemagne was crowned). Empire and papacy should be in harmony—as "the two cherubim facing each other with wings conjoined over the mercy seat . . . the two great lights which God set in the firmament of heaven, the greater light (the papacy) to rule the day, the lesser light (the empire) to rule the night." Empire and papacy were the two swords of the Apostles—"behold here are two swords" (Luke xxii, 38).

But, Innocent went on, the princes had exceeded their legitimate powers in proclaiming Philip emperor. The legal mind of Innocent would not allow that an emperor could be chosen by Teutonic princes. It was for them, he pointed out, to choose their king—the king of the Romans—it was for the pope to make that king emperor. Not till two years had passed did Innocent declare his decision. It was for Otto of Brunswick. In the *Deliberation on the question of the Empire,* the pope gave his reasons for deciding in favour of Otto. The boy-king of the Sicilies, Frederick, was too young. Philip of Swabia was still excommunicate—under sentence of Pope Celestine—for the evil he had done against the Church, and for that evil he had neither made amends nor showed repentance. Philip's family had persistently opposed the Church. The empire was not an hereditary possession of the Hohenstaufen; to make Philip emperor would, as a matter of fact, turn the empire into a property of the family, since he would be the fourth Hohenstaufen in succession. Therefore Otto, the pope decides, must be proclaimed emperor. It is Otto whom the pope recognises as king and it is to Otto all men are commanded to swear loyalty and obedience. In answer to remonstrances from the party of Philip, Innocent carefully explained that it was no temporal jurisdiction the pope exercised, except indirectly. The pope could not override the electoral system of the empire, he could only declare through his legate, who was not himself an elector, the worthiness of the emperor, and only in disputed elections judge, confirm, and decide on the elected candidate. Otto was the worthier candidate. "No king could rightly reign unless he devoutly served Christ's vicar," for "kings but rule over their respective kingdoms while the pope rules over the whole world."

But Innocent does not say a king may not *lawfully* reign if he is anti-papal; he cannot *rightly* reign. The distinction is no mere matter of words, no verbal nicety or legal quibble. The king of the Romans properly elected is the lawful king whatever his attitude to the papacy. But he will not reign rightly or justly unless, crowned by the pope, he serves as emperor the pope in things temporal for the promotion of things spiritual and eternal: An emperor reigning in opposition to the pope implied the reign of unrightness, of injustice. The imperial rule of the Hohenstaufens had in fact borne harshly and unjustly on the popes and the Christian people of God. Philip of Swabia had aided and abetted his imperial brother Henry in the ravaging of the States of the Church. He was still under sentence of excommunication. In Otto of Brunswick Pope

Innocent placed his hopes for the peace of Christendom.
He was not to see these hopes fulfilled.

Innocent Supports Otto of Brunswick

The papal decision was completely ignored. Philip and Otto went on with their war while fifty German bishops, in assembly at Bamberg, declared that Philip was their emperor, and that as for the pope, he was always the enemy of Germany—a cry that would be raised again by Martin Luther in the centuries to come. So thoroughly were these episcopal vassals of the Hohenstaufen saturated with the doctrine of imperial supremacy that, looking back on the bad days before Pope Gregory VII had restored the papal independence of the empire, they declared the emperor should name the pope, not the pope the emperor. Of course, they were excommunicated, these fifty bishops, for thus flagrantly disregarding canonical oaths of obedience to the pope, only pouring contempt on all ecclesiastical obedience and doing violence to canon law. The bishops took no more notice of Innocent's sentence than Philip had taken. Neither would they budge from their palaces nor surrender their estates. When the pope consecrated new bishops to fill the sees declared vacant, the faithful in Germany had the spectacle of rival bishops in some fifty sees, Catholic bishops not in disagreement about articles of faith, but bitterly divided on the political issue. As if it were not enough that rival emperors should lay waste the lands of Germany, anarchy, robbery, and murder following in the destructive train of war, the very episcopate brought disruptive schism into the Church of God, leaving the plain man in perplexity as to who was the true bishop and true priest, who the intruder.

And yet those very years of the war of Philip and Otto for the imperial throne, with all the miseries entailed, were the period of amazing fruitfulness in the history of German letters.

The creative period of the *Minnesingers,* with outpouring of lyrics, the period of the composition of the great German epics that told the legends of the Niebelungenlied, of *Parsifal,* of *Tristan and Isolde.*

Philip and Otto went on with their war, every year bringing military gains to the Hohenstaufen and defection among Otto's supporters. Pope Innocent could only watch the conflict, urging the combatants by numerous embassies to make peace; but noting at the same time the steady decline in Otto's fortunes. Sooner or later Otto must be utterly defeated and Philip be left undisputed emperor. For the sake of peace in Germany, Innocent gradually prepared to acknowledge Philip and to persuade Otto to withdraw. Otto was the papal candidate, not Philip the Hohenstaufen, but the statesmanship of Innocent accepted the facts—the defeat of the papal candidate and the ruin of his cause. The inability of Otto to reign as emperor; the horror of this civil war with its destruction of life, waste of temporal goods, ruin and degradation of immortal souls, and fostering of hate, moved Innocent as he saw the approaching downfall of the man of his choice to hasten the coming of peace and to induce an armistice.

Statesman of Europe, Innocent, without petulance or reproach at the failure of his policy, allowing no sense of personal disappointment to warp the responsibility that belonged to the vicar of Christ, unhurriedly prepared to take the second best, since the first was denied. In politics throughout the centuries the wiser statesmen know when compromise is necessary, when opportunism decrees the adoption of the second best. It must frequently be so if the end pursued is to be attained. The end for Innocent was peace, with an emperor acknowledged by the empire. If Christendom was to be saved not only from disintegrating anarchy within, but from Islam and heresy encroaching from without there must be an emperor. Otto had failed to win allegiance, he had been shamefully deserted by many who had hailed him king. It was only a matter of time before Philip would be completely victorious.

For his part Philip was anxious to come to terms with the pope. After Adolf, archbishop of Cologne, to whom the office belonged, had solemnly crowned him at Aix-la-Chapelle in January, 1205,[15] Philip wrote an earnest appeal to Innocent, setting out his claims against Otto and avowing his loyalty to the pope.

So far from being ill-disposed to the holy Roman Church, Philip acknowledged it as the mother and mistress of all churches; willingly he honoured it, whole-heartedly he accepted the pope's full authority in matters of religion. For the defence of the Roman Church he would fight, for its supremacy he would strive. If the pope only knew the truth about him, knew his real devotion to the Holy See, Philip was sure the pope would take him to his heart.

All this, of course, was very gratifying, but peace was the immediate necessity. Innocent again sent papal legates to arrange a truce, and though Otto with his dwindling remnant of followers and his cause obviously lost, still stuck out for the kingship the legates did at last succeed in getting a truce proclaimed for a year. Everywhere the truce was well received for even the princes were tired of the civil war. Innocent now released Philip from the ban of excommunication, and acknowledged him as the feudal lord of the Hohenstaufen territories in Italy. Yet Innocent still treated Otto as "emperor-elect," still wrote of him as "king," though the end of his career was, it seemed to all, in sight.

And then, just when the prospect of Philip's sovereignty

---

[15] It was inexcusable, Innocent declared, this act of Archbishop Adolf. He had pledged himself to Otto and openly disregarding the pope's decision had violated his word. The archbishop took no notice of Innocent's rebuke nor of the excommunication that followed.

was at its brightest, with an emperor acceptable to pope and princes about to be seated on the imperial throne, the Hohenstaufen was murdered at Bamberg by one of his own party, Otto of Wittelsbach, Count of Bavaria. It was an act of personal vengeance. (Otto felt himself insulted because Philip first promised him his daughter in marriage and then married her to some one else.) There was talk and gossip of a conspiracy, but not the slightest evidence. Private hate and nothing else was the cause of the murder that altered so completely for a time the position of things in Germany, and gave Otto of Brunswick in the very hour of his defeat the crown he coveted. All opposition ceased on Philip's death. There was no longer an Hohenstaufen candidate in the field. Bishops and princes were sick of the civil war and the fast-spreading anarchy. Otto the Guelph, indubitably emperor, was re-elected king at a great diet at Frankfort in November, 1208. Innocent wrote of the high hopes born of Otto's unchallenged election. Now surely would pope and emperor reign in harmony, Innocent declared in a long and affectionate letter to Otto. They had never met, but Innocent was persuaded that in Otto he had found an emperor after his own heart, one to whom the government of the world had been so manifestly awarded. Let them remain in unity seeking righteousness. Then, ruling with the two swords committed to them, the spiritual and the temporal, how great would be the good that would follow, greater than words can tell. Such a concord would be invincible. "Pope and Emperor, reigning with common purpose, the words of the prophet shall be fulfilled; the sun and moon now fixed in their orbits, the crooked paths shall be made straight and the rough ways plain." In further token of good will Innocent quashed by dispensation all legal impediments to Otto's marriage with Philip of Swabia's daughter Beatrice—they were related within the prohibited degrees.

Otto Sole Emperor

Never was there fairer prospect of peace than in that first year of Otto's sovereignty, never Innocent more hopeful of that reconciliation of pope and emperor that would bring comfort and healing to Christendom. Of course, Otto must needs go to Rome to be crowned by the pope, and his vows and pledges, his oaths and promises to the Holy See to do right by the pope, were given apparently in all honesty in his setting out. Yet vows and pledges, oaths and promises alike came to nothing, and within a year the concord so warmly acclaimed by Innocent was broken utterly.

At Spires, in March, Otto took the oath of obedience to the Holy See in things spiritual, going out of his way to express in gratitude to God his desire to do all that was right by the Church. The clergy should be free throughout the empire to elect the cathedral chapters, the cathedral chapters to nominate the bishops. No hindrance on the emperor's part would check the right of appeal to Rome. On the temporal side the emperor would do his best to root up all heresy from his dominions.

Once more Innocent writes to Otto on the relations of pope and emperor, for "the rule of the world is chiefly entrusted to us two." The Roman pontiff is the more anxious for the greater glory of the Empire because he it is who confers the imperial crown. The Church needs an emperor and has no wish to be without one; for if pope and emperor are the two great lights set in the firmament (the sun, the pope; the moon, the emperor), "when the moon is eclipsed darkness becomes darker still," and for want of an emperor "the wild violence of heretics and pagans cruelly increases to the great hurt of faithful people." Innocent stresses the case for a strong empire — since "the Church desires a devoted defender, the whole empire is in need of a careful guardian." At the same time Innocent reiterates the former teaching—*sacerdotium*, the power of the papacy is of God, *regnum*, the imperial power is of man's creation.

In the autumn Otto entered Italy with a large army and a host of retainers. At Viterbo for the first time pope and emperor met face to face. On both sides the most cordial and affectionate greetings were expressed. How often, Otto had written, he had longed to see the pope! "In thee my heart finds its delight," were the words of Innocent to his imperial guest. With elaborate rejoicings and much pageantry Otto was made welcome in the States of the Church.

Far different was it when he came to Rome. In Rome the citizens were determined to show themselves as offensive and disagreeable to the emperor as their neighbours at Viterbo had been amiable. It has been said they were aggrieved, these Roman citizens, because they had not been consulted concerning the date of the emperor's coronation, but whatever the reason they were ready to give the emperor an unpleasant reception. Innocent knew but too well that when the ill-tempered mood was on them, his Romans would make riot and disorder; especially when they could do it at the expense of foreigners, of Germans whom they held in hatred, traditional hatred, stored up and easily exploded. There was, of course, no valid reason at all for treating Otto, the Guelph, as an enemy. So far he had been in the opposite camp to the Hohenstaufen, and he came to Rome as one approved by the pope and with the pope's blessing. The citizens were out to make trouble; all that Innocent could do was to thwart the malignant purpose of his wayward and undisciplined children.

Otto, with his army, encamped on Monte Mario, north of the Vatican and beyond the walls two days before the coronation. Had the emperor's men been content to stay there, outside the city, all might have been well. Unfortunately, yet very naturally, some of the Teutonic officers, quite important persons from Augsburg, thought it a good opportunity to see something of Rome of which they had heard so much. Little they saw, for the Roman mob, choosing to take offence at the manners of these foreigners, fell upon them; swords were drawn, blows given, more than one German killed. A bad beginning, this scandal of a lawless, violent mob within the pope's own city.

On the first Sunday in October came the day for Otto's coronation. To prevent any hostile incursion by the Roman mob, imperial troops were sent to hold the bridge of St. Angelo, and through the dense crowd that had gathered on the road from Monte Mario to the Vatican a passage was cleared for the emperor and his immense retinue. This was done by scattering money to the right and left of the road for the people to scramble for, and by an escort of imperial soldiers making use of their pikes to push back the spectators and let the procession get through. On the threshold of St. Peter's, Otto took the oath prescribed for the occasion, the oath that made him the sworn protector of the Church and of the poor, and then within the historic basilica he was duly crowned by the pope, with all the ceremonial that pertained to the solemn function. The coronation over, Otto carrying out the traditional duty of helping the pope to mount his horse, pope and emperor adjourned to the Vatican palace hard by, where the official banquet was held at the imperial expense and all who would, rich and poor alike, were freely entertained.

So far on that memorable day everything passed off without a hitch, all the customary rites and ceremonies carefully performed, the proceedings unmarred by interruption. By nightfall a wild and savage onslaught by the Romans left the emperor with many of his soldiers killed and deprived of more than a thousand horses, to say nothing of a vast amount of stores and luggage. Battle and murder marked the end of the day of Otto's coronation.

Hostility in Rome

The attack was made on the imperial forces as the procession, on its way back to Monte Mario, reached the boundaries of the old Leonine city. Some said the Germans had made insulting remarks about the Romans. Others that the emperor, refusing to distribute money which the people expected to receive, had enraged the mob. One contemporary writer declares that Otto at the official banquet had said something about recovering all the lands that had once been in the emperor's possession, and this speech had made the Romans angry. Innocent had brought the citizens of Rome to keep peace within the city and among themselves—how many years it had taken!—he could not restrain a lawless, excitable mob from making war on foreigners.

In the popular mind violence was entirely justified. A German emperor who came to Rome to be crowned and was mean in his benefactions—why shouldn't he be plundered? Were they, citizens of imperial Rome, to put up with insults from German officers? Such shabby conduct on the part of the emperor, such arrogance on the part of his subordinates, were altogether too much for the citizens of imperial Rome, altogether intolerable and not to be endured. So they fell upon Otto's grand retinue and left the emperor despoiled. The emperor, not without reason, was also left in a state of high indignation.

Innocent, anxious to stop further fighting, aware that the Romans having got away with so much plunder would be only too ready to fight for more, urged the emperor not to stay any longer at Monte Mario, but to depart from the neighbourhood of Rome as quickly as possible.

For a while Otto refused to stir. He demanded compensation for his losses, protested that he had been robbed and that reparation must be made. When it was obvious that the Roman mob had no intention to disgorge its plunder, no less obvious that supplies of food were running short, Otto moved from Monte Mario and halting some ten miles to the northwest of Rome wrote to Innocent proposing a conference. It was said that at the coronation banquet Otto had brought up the question of the overlordship of lands in Tuscany given to the papacy by the duchess Matilda, that devoted ally of the popes in the time of Hildebrand. Now, Otto suggested, if the pope and he came together—for his part he was willing to return to Rome at the risk of being killed by the populace, if the pope couldn't come to him—this would be an excellent opportunity for a settlement of all questions in dispute.

Innocent knowing only too well that the return of the emperor to Rome, or his own departure from the city, would be the signal for a renewal of riot and disorder by the mob, replied that the better plan was for envoys to meet, and thus an honourable agreement acceptable to both of them concerning questions of territory could surely be effected. Otto, constitutionally incapable of keeping promises, seeing himself at last emperor unopposed, absolutely supreme, solemnly crowned, thought no more of the pope's words on the relation of pope and emperor than of the oaths he had taken before the coronation. Power was his, power and yet more power would he have—till he fell.

Through Tuscany, through the duchy of Spoleto and the march of Ancona, Otto moved triumphantly with his army, treating the States of the Church as possessions of the empire. Then he turned his attention to the kingdom of the Sicilies, encouraged by more than one of the nobles who professed loyalty to the boy-king, Frederick; notably by Diepold of Acerra who, thinking it an excellent opportunity to improve his position, again transferred his allegiance and renounced his oaths. Joining the emperor seemed a far more profitable course to Diepold than standing by his sovereign, so young, a mere child, so weak in arms.

Whatever the lawyers might say concerning the overlordship of the States of the Church, some arguing that in temporals the emperor was the supreme governor, others that the pope in temporals no less than spirituals was master in his own dominions, Otto had no shadow of claim to the Sicilian kingdom. All that southern part of Italy we call Naples, with the island of Sicily, was Norman property. Constance had brought it to the emperor Henry on her marriage. Never had these lands belonged to the Hohenstaufen family, never were they a part of the imperial territories. Constance deliberately placed the Sicilies under the feudal over lordship of the pope, so that on her death her youthful son would have a strong protector. Otto, ignoring all protests, disregarding the appeal of Frederick who offered money and the withdrawal of all his claims to the German crown, marched into Naples and settled himself at Capua. To Innocent's remonstrances (in the bitterness of his soul, he wrote to the archbishop of Ravenna repenting that he had made Otto emperor) there was no reply. Otto, the emperor, acknowledged no superior.

Innocent, knowing too well that an emperor ruling in the Sicilies had shut in the Pope and left him politically a prisoner, prepared to make an end of this outrageous conduct. There was more than political subjection of the papacy to be considered. Innocent held the sacred trust committed to him by Constance, the widowed queen. He, chief shepherd of Christendom, was explicitly the guardian of orphans. Constance had made him feudal overlord of the Sicilies that her orphan son, Frederick, might not be left at the mercy of robber barons and imperialist cutthroats. The responsibility had been laid upon him. Pope Innocent was not the man to evade responsibility, to shirk duty. The orphan Frederick must not be sacrificed to the ambitions of the German emperor. Otto must be brought to reason, must be compelled to cease from his campaign of annexation.

But Otto, settled at Capua, enjoying power, declined all the pope's invitations to amend his ways. In adversity Otto never admitted defeat. In his worst moments he clung to the hope of better days and fought on when all seemed lost. Now in the hour of prosperity he was undone, ruined by absolute power and by the servility of followers. Pope Innocent and his warnings and remonstrances went for nothing to Otto, then enjoying life at Capua. After the cold and fog of north Germany, the warmth and sunshine of Capua were irresistible. Otto boasted that he would have all the Sicilies for his own, and so far as the mainland was concerned the boast was not vainly made. There were days when it seemed to the anxious youthful Frederick that the only chance of escape from Otto was to fly to sanctuary with the Saracens.

Otto dallied too long at Capua. During his absence from Germany indifference succeeded regard, personal loyalty grew cold. When at last all the pope's appeals to him had failed (and Innocent went so far as to write that if the emperor would give up this invasion of the Sicilies his treatment of the States of the Church should not be brought against him) and the solemn excommunication was pronounced that placed Otto outside the pale of Christian fellowship, no protest came from Germany.

Otto Excommunicated

Otto affected to despise the excommunication, repeating his boast that he would drive Frederick from the island of Sicily and would have his revenge on Philip of France, since Philip had always been against him and against his English uncle, King John. But the sands were running out even when he wrote in this high imperial strain.

Full twelve months passed before the excommunication was solemnly proclaimed throughout the empire. The respite was ignored by Otto, still bent on Sicilian conquests, deaf to Innocent's final appeals to be content with his imperial territories, satisfied that he was invincible. Now that Otto was in the face of all Europe pronounced a "heretic," his subjects released from allegiance to him, the next thing was to look for his successor.

Innocent, with every hope in Otto gone, knowing it was necessary to have this oath-breaking, tyrannical, and altogether dangerous emperor deposed, turned for help to Philip Augustus of France. Philip had been troublesome enough with his matrimonial irregularities, but Innocent recognised his abilities, his statesmanship, his services to France. Philip had also warned the pope that Otto was the wrong man for emperor, that Otto would never go on crusade, in fact, that Otto had no ideas beyond annexing other people's property and making himself supreme ruler in Europe. Frankly Innocent wrote to Philip of his bitter disappointment in Otto, regretting that he had not taken the French king's warning to heart and reminding himself that God had regretted that he had made Saul king. Innocent added that Otto's threats against France had not moved him, he had answered these threats with the statement that no papal support would be given to such a campaign.

Invited by Innocent's letters to elect a successor to the excommunicated Otto, princes and dukes of the empire met at Nuremberg and there and then declared Frederick to be their choice. Innocent endorsed the election. Much as he distrusted the Hohenstaufens, remembering all their hurt to the papacy in the past, there was no alternative. Otto had proved a worse enemy than the Hohenstaufen; he never was anything but a fighting man of large ambitions by whom any promise might be broken, any vow ignored if it no longer suited his warlike policy.

A remnant of Otto's supporters in Germany, when

Frederick was elected, at once started a civil war urging the deposed emperor to return at once before all was lost. As a matter of fact Otto's cause was lost before he reached Germany in the spring of 1212. The long delay at Capua, the days and nights spent on planning the conquest of the Sicilies were his utter undoing. Hardly had he crossed the Alps to return to Germany when the youthful Frederick came to Rome. The Roman citizens gave him an enthusiastic welcome. Innocent received him with the greatest cordiality. So young, so full of courage, so willing to listen to the wise words of the pope—how could Innocent not be persuaded that at last here was the emperor of his desire?

All that was possible for Frederick's safe journey to Germany was done by Innocent. He gave him money, he found him a fleet of ships to carry him to Genoa, with a cardinal legate to accompany him, besides writing numerous letters on his behalf. Opposition from Milan and the communes of Lombardy, where bitter memories of the tyranny of Barbarossa made hateful the thought of another Hohenstaufen emperor, was evaded, plots of Otto's mercenaries to waylay the "youth from Sicily" were escaped.

Election of Frederick II

Frederick reached Frankfort—to be proclaimed emperor-elect by the Teutonic princes, at a great gathering of knights and nobles. For, in addition to the papal delegates, Philip of France was there with some five thousand horsemen. Frederick had already joined Philip in alliance offensive and defensive, and with money from Philip he bought the support of many a prince of the empire who otherwise would have held aloof.

Otto saw his cause ruined, yet in his retirement in Brunswick he made ready to strike one more blow at his enemies. Rally the princes of Germany to his support he could not. They were already bought and Otto had no money. King John of England, still anxious to destroy the power of France, sent him troops and with these and his own Brunswickers Otto prepared to do battle with Philip. At Bouvines in Flanders, on July 27, 1214, a decisive action was fought; it ended in Otto's defeat, destroying finally all hope of recovering the imperial throne. Nothing was left for Otto but to live out the rest of his days in Brunswick, while Frederick, crowned at Aachen, was indisputably emperor. Otto survived Pope Innocent by two years and died a penitent man. But not till death was close upon him was Otto reconciled to the Church whose authority he had so long despised.

Frederick, on the threshold of manhood, made many declarations of loyalty and obedience to Pope Innocent. After Otto was dead he revealed the character that was to astonish Europe and gain the title *stupor mundi*. But whatever his professions of love and duty to Innocent, one thing is certain, Frederick II from the day of his coronation never saw himself as the lesser luminary in heaven, with the pope as the greater. He would be no moon to the sun of the papacy. Grandson of Barbarossa, a true Hohenstaufen, this amazing young man was for thirty years to trample papal claims and terrify Christendom by his superb imperialism.

Innocent could not have foreseen the ruin and disaster that would follow the election of Frederick II. He could not foresee the defection of Otto. The vision, that was always before Innocent, of the two swords wielded by pope and emperor was never to be fulfilled, neither in his lifetime nor in the time to come. Yet before he died Innocent could take comfort from the assurances of Frederick that all should be well with the Church and no harm come to the Holy See; that the clergy should be free from imperial constraint at elections and in their appeals to Rome; that all that had been taken from the Church by his predecessors should be restored, heretics no longer be allowed to intrude on the faithful. Innocent was "father and lord" to Frederick in the last golden bull issued by the emperor, "king of the Romans by the grace of God and the Pope," as he styled himself. Innocent lying mortally sick at Perugia may not have read this bull. It did but confirm the many promises made by Frederick to the pope who had befriended him from childhood, protected him from enemies, aided him when things in Sicily were at their worst, and brought him in early manhood to the imperial throne. But Frederick was incalculable alike in his dealings with popes and princes. No whisper of the emperor's future policy fell on the dying ears of Innocent.

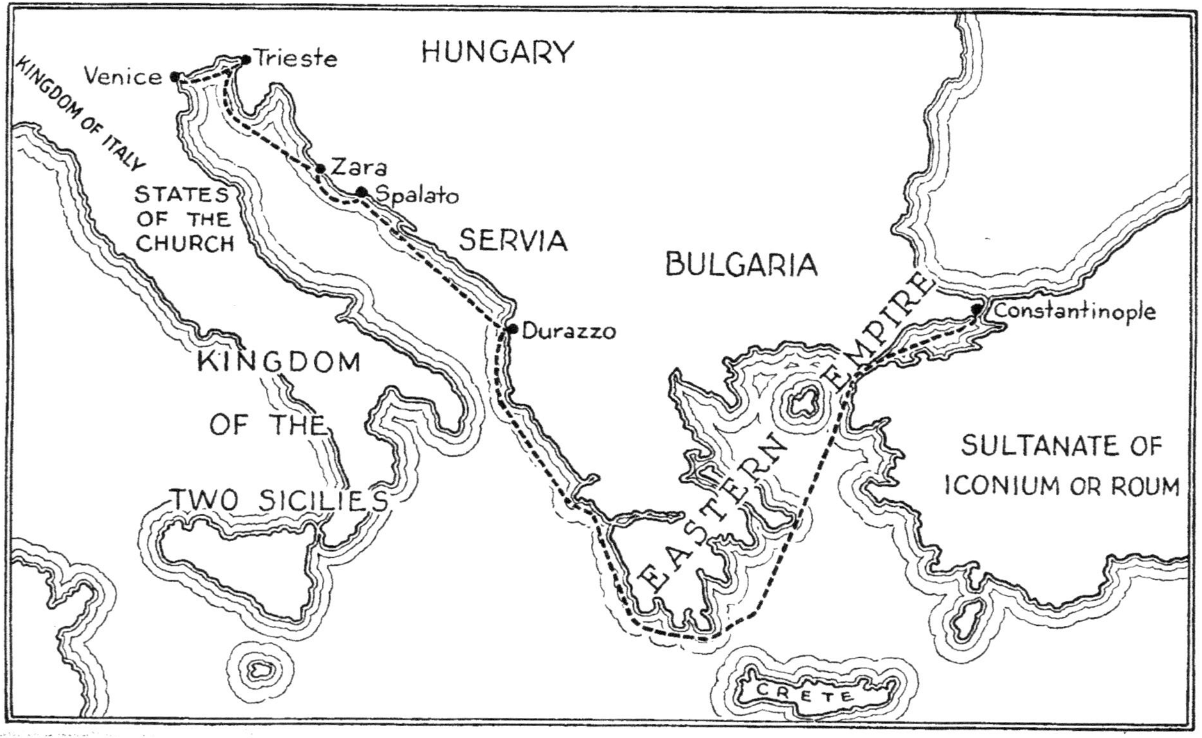
HUNGARY
KINGDOM OF ITALY
Venice
Trieste
Zara
Spalato
STATES OF THE CHURCH
SERVIA
BULGARIA
Durazzo
Constantinople
KINGDOM OF THE TWO SICILIES
EASTERN EMPIRE
SULTANATE OF ICONIUM OR ROUM
CRETE

CHAPTER VI
Pope Innocent and the Crusades

Fourth Crusade—Diversion to Constantinople—Sack of Constantinople—The Children's Crusade.

THE conflict of pope and emperor is the major political issue in medieval Europe. The crusades, these recurring wars of Christians and Mohammedans for possession of the holy places in Palestine, are for all Europe the supreme vital struggle of the Middle Ages. They transcend all internal strife, the crusades, fought by Christians to keep back the advancing armies of Islam; a War of Europe against Asia, of Christendom against the sons of the Prophet, of the cross against the crescent; waged on both sides with all the ferocity of a holy war, illuminated from time to time by incidents of rare chivalry, by deeds of noble charity.

The long effort to keep the Moslem power out of Europe, to save Christendom from subjection to the Turk, continued after the close of the Middle Ages, lasting indeed in the Balkan peninsula to modern times.

Innocent III inherited the crusades as he inherited the papal conflict with the empire. He realised the magnitude of this campaign for mastery in the Near East, and with foresight of the statesman saw the advancing tide of Islam, knew the divisions of Christians greatly assisted that advance, called on the princes of Christendom to heal their feuds and resist the encroaching religion, the subversive alien rule of the Asiatic.

The fatal weakness in all plans for the defeat of Islam was the dissension in the Christian forces. Irreconcilable divisions, fostered by pride and avarice, turned the arms of the great military orders, Templars and Hospitallers, against one another in Palestine, set bishop in opposition to bishop, kept kings and princes in pursuit of personal gain wasting their strength on mutual destruction. Not the superiority of the Moslem armies, but the sheer want of unity amongst Christians brought the defeat of the crusades and the loss of Palestine. Innocent, forever working to overthrow the Mohammedan power, was frustrated by the discordant warring elements that made up the hosts of the cross and flouted the papal authority.

At the very outset of Innocent's reign Richard of England and Philip Augustus of France, crusaders both, were in mortal opposition. King Richard of the Lion-heart, bent on recovering lands in France that Philip was not at all inclined to surrender, boasted that when he had won back from the French what he maintained were lawfully his then would he once more set out to overthrow the Saracen. (Henry VI, Hohenstaufen emperor, had distinguished himself by the capture and imprisonment of Richard on the latter's return from the crusades, and Philip Augustus saw that for France the right policy was alliance with the Hohenstaufen. Besides Philip was tired of the feudal and family claims of English kings to lands in France.) John, on Richard's death, resumed hostilities with Philip, enmity between France and England became traditional with the inevitable result that the cause of Islam prospered at the expense of Christendom and the peace of Europe was destroyed. Neither from France nor England could Innocent look for leadership in the crusade he planned. At the best he could only hope for money. Less hope could be discerned from the empire, with Philip of Swabia and Otto of Brunswick in deadly civil war.

In vain Innocent remonstrated, warned and rebuked

Christian princes and prelates in the Near East, exhorting them in the name of their holy religion to refrain from injuring one another, urging them to the defence of their common faith. Templars and Hospitallers, enervated—slowly, imperceptibly corrupted by long residence in Palestine, were found on opposite sides in a war to settle the question of the reigning dynasty in Antioch, the Templars fighting side by side with Moslems for one prince while the Hospitaller allied with the Armenians fought for his rival candidate. Many letters Innocent wrote to bring all Christians together, appealing to the king of Armenia not to antagonise the Templars, to the Hospitallers to settle their differences with the Templars by law rather than by force of arms. The Latin kingdom of Jerusalem had gone down before the might of Saladin and his armies, but the sea-coast of Palestine was still held by the crusaders and Saladin was dead. The prospect, bleak in Innocent's eyes, was not hopeless. Writing to his legate, the patriarch of Jerusalem, the pope deplored the crimes committed in Palestine by Christians, "Christians only in name." Worse than the infidel, Innocent described them, were "these wretched Christians who betrayed one another, hated one another, and scandalised one another." Nor did he hesitate to appeal to the Moslem sultan of Aleppo—"though you have not yet embraced the Christian faith we learn that you have veneration for it"—to protect the Latin patriarch of Antioch from the violence of Behemond, Christian prince of Tripoli, who having made himself, with the aid of Templars and Moslems, prince of Antioch, had proceeded to throw the Latin patriarch into prison, where he died, and then to intrude a Greek patriarch in his room. (To the remonstrance of Innocent's legate at such conduct Behemond replied, quite falsely, that his emperor at Constantinople had authority from the pope to exempt the prince of Antioch from all ecclesiastical courts.)

Bleak prospect the recovery of the Holy Land, with the

Moslem power already established in north Africa and in a great part of Spain, with Moslem philosophy and doctrine finding receptive minds, so that Moslem influence in art and letters must be taken into serious account in the story of the fashioning of medieval Europe!

The enfeebled empire of the East, the Greek emperor at Constantinople, a far weaker personage than Innocent held him to be, increased the difficulties of the crusades.

In the mind of Innocent, Christian unity was fundamental—one Lord, one Faith, one Baptism, the Christian teaching. He saw in the gospel of Christ the expressed doctrine of the one Fold and the one Shepherd. Yet the emperor at Constantinople and his patriarch would not come into the Fold, but persisted in finding arguments for remaining as they were, clinging to the fragments of the Roman empire of the east, jealous of the supremacy of Rome in things spiritual and temporal.

The independent republic of Venice was another stumbling-block. Thoroughly Christian and Catholic, this Venetian oligarchy of merchants, was nonetheless always ready to trade with Moslems, to supply them with armaments and in fact, from a business point of view, made a very good thing out of the crusades. As far as Venice was concerned the prosperity of Venice came first; the sacred cause of the cross versus the crescent was quite a secondary matter. All of them, Christian princes in Europe, Christian forces in Palestine, Greek emperor and patriarch in Constantinople, Venetian republic, mocked and confounded Innocent's conception of a fresh crusade for the recovery of the Holy Land. The pope's heart was set on this recovery, to that end his powers were directed—his Christian subjects decided otherwise.

Fourth Crusade

The fourth crusade was instigated by Innocent and inspired by the preaching of various French priests. The sermons of Fulk, parish priest of Neuilly, were particularly effective in creating an enthusiasm for the holy war. Innocent succeeded in persuading Richard of England, and Philip of France to agree to a five-year truce — Richard died within a few months of the agreement. Further, and this was a more difficult task, they were to raise money by a tax of one fortieth on all ecclesiastical revenues for one year. From Germany, already the scene of civil war between Otto and Philip of Swabia, nothing could be got. The fourth crusade was therefore predominantly French. The king declined to leave France a second time for the East, but great feudal lords, Baldwin of Flanders, Theobald of Champagne, Louis of Blois, Boniface of Montferrat, with Simon of Montfort, solemnly took the cross and prepared to march with their dependents. Theobald of Champagne was the chosen leader, and on his early death (1201) Boniface, marquis of Montferrat, succeeded to the command. Boniface was a cousin of Philip of Swabia, Philip of Swabia was the son-in-law of the Byzantine Emperor Isaac Angelus, whom his brother Alexis III had blinded, deposed, and thrown into prison. Isaac's son, the future Alexis IV, escaping from prison, pleaded to Boniface for vengeance and so the fourth crusade was diverted to Constantinople to serve, as it was thought, the interests of the Hohenstaufen. In fact, the fourth crusade, Innocent's cherished plan, was sacrificed to the Hohenstaufen policy and the commercial gains of the Venetian republic. Innocent, never fully aware of the agreements made between Boniface and Venice, had misgivings, misgivings that increased with every fresh item of news that reached him.

From Villehardouin, the French historian who accompanied the crusade, can be learnt the events of those years —1202-1204 — that saw the capture of Constantinople, the destruction of the Eastern empire, the setting up of a Latin empire that was to last for nearly sixty years, and the unexpected end of Innocent's hopes and plans.[16]

It was a hard bargain the doge of Venice, Henry Dandalo, an old man and blind, but shrewd and vigorous—heroic in the eyes of the contemporaries—drove with the leaders of the crusades before any start could be made. In return for 85,000 marks (about £200,000) the Venetians agreed to provide ships for the voyage and provisions for 35,000 men for nine months. Egypt was to be the objective since at that time a truce existed in Palestine between Moslems and Christians. Innocent confirmed the agreement conditionally. A papal legate must go with the crusaders and there must be no injuries to other Christian bodies unless the crusaders were first attacked. Suspicion of intrigues at Constantinople disturbed Innocent's mind, for Alexis IV had already implored the pope to take up his case against the "wicked uncle" who reigned as emperor, and Boniface soon followed, mumbling words that Innocent met with emphatic refusal to countenance any change of route.

When the crusaders assembled at Venice they were short of their numbers, and what made it more embarrassing, short of the money they had promised. Dandalo showed them a way out of the financial crisis. The port of Zara on the Dalmatian coast, which belonged to the king of Hungary but had once belonged to Venice, ought to return to its former allegiance. Let the crusaders restore Zara to Venice and Dandalo would remit the balance of the passage money. Rumours of an attack on Zara reached Innocent and he threatened with excommunication all who should take part in so shameful a thing, for the king of Hungary had himself taken the cross.

Boniface, marquis of Montferrat, prudently kept out of the way while the agreement was made; Simon of Mont- fort declined to act against the pope's orders when he learnt of the

---

[16] Consult *L'Eglise et l'Orient au Moyen Age — Les Croisades,* by Louis Brehier. Fifth ed., Paris, 1928.

papal prohibition; but the rest of the French leaders, in horrible perplexity, for the doge kept them more or less prisoners on the Lido until the day of sailing, consented to the terms.

A month after leaving Venice the crusaders arrived at Zara to be met by its citizens with letters from Rome threatening papal excommunication on all who made war on the city. The Venetians cared nothing for papal excommunications—but they were not told of the papal letters—the prosperity of Venice was their heart's desire. Momentary hesitation vanished at the call to the capture and plunder of this rich city. Zara fell to the crusaders. Venice held once more the capital of Dalmatia, the only port that challenged the supremacy of the republic in the Adriatic.

In the face of the stern disapproval of the pope this had been done. Innocent, on hearing that Zara had been stormed and captured, excommunicated the crusaders for the violation of the terms he had strictly enjoined, and Boniface and the rest of the French leaders found themselves in an awkward position. To proceed, under the ban of the Church, on the crusade was altogether out of order. The bulk of the army was made up of stout fighting men, men of manifest sincerity who had enlisted under their respective lords in the assurance that the crusade was a holy war, that all taking part in it earned the promised indulgence. Now they heard they were excommunicated, cut off from the fellowship of the Church. Of course, they put the blame on the Venetians. Messengers were sent off to the pope to ask forgiveness and at the same time to explain that the taking of Zara had been done under pressure of the Venetians. They were forgiven, these soldiers of the cross — Innocent was forever forgiving and absolving the recalcitrant, penitent children when they expressed sorrow—but grief and indignation filled his letters. In making war on Zara they had taken their hands from the plough, turning away from the pure intention; now the gold was turned to dross, the silver blackened. The devil, the old enemy of mankind, had infected them all with some portion of the leaven of injustice. The devil had made them turn their arms against their brethren, knowing that man can show no greater love for man than by laying down his life for him, and thereby excluding them from the reward of that great love.

Boniface, Baldwin, Count of Flanders, Louis of Blois and the other commanders, followed up the path of reconciliation by sending many expressions of regret and promises of future obedience. One and all these leaders confessed they had not let the Venetians know of the papal prohibition concerning attacks on fellow Christians for the simple reason that the Venetians, had they known, would have refused all further use of their ships.

Innocent in reply pointed out the harm that had been done to the cause of the crusade, the cause the pope had laboured for. It discouraged Christians from taking the cross and supplied the Saracens with fresh hope when Christians fought with Christians. Let them in future on no account do injury to the land of the Greeks, let them not be led away by any notion of Greek indifference to the Holy See, or any talk of a usurping emperor at Constantinople.

The pope might say what he liked, the Venetians had no intention of altering their plans. Innocent took it for granted that the objective of the crusaders was Egypt, for that was the original strategy — Alexandria to be the base of the war in Palestine — and he waited patiently for news.

Diversion to Constantinople

When the news reached him it was of a startling and disturbing nature. Instead of sailing to Egypt, the fleet—and those who saw the ships provided by the Venetians were full of admiration at the size and equipment of the vessels—went directly to Constantinople. Dandalo and Boniface were bent on taking Constantinople, the rest of the crusaders obeyed the orders of their chiefs—except Simon of Mont- fort and his followers who would have nothing to do with the enterprise, departing in their own ships to the coast of Palestine.

The Venetians and Boniface favoured the Hohenstaufen policy, but Dandalo saw in the removal of the Greek emperor and the setting up of a Latin the prospect of far better trading conditions. None of the French chiefs had strength or energy to gainsay the doge, that masterful old man who, with personal animosity spurring him to overthrow the empire of the Greeks, was the driving force of this unhappy fourth crusade. In the summer of 1203 Constantinople was taken without any formidable opposition from its defenders, Alexis III fled from the city and Alexis IV was crowned co-emperor with his blind father Isaac Angelus.

Communications between Constantinople and Rome were slow and difficult, and while Innocent had every reason to believe the crusaders had gone to Egypt no news reached him for months; not until Alexis IV and certain of the crusaders wrote to him of what had taken place. Faced with the accomplished fact, carried out by the contumacious Venetians in complete disregard of papal commands. Innocent had to make the best of a bad business.

Worse was to follow.

Of course, many letters came from Constantinople to Innocent, letters of apology and explanation concerning the diversion of the crusade from Egypt. Alexis IV laid great stress on his desire to serve the pope "Catholic successor of the Prince of the Apostles" and to persuade the Eastern churches to follow his example. The crusaders wrote that, reduced to poverty, they were in no condition to proceed to the Holy Land, before they had placed Alexis IV, their paymaster, on his throne. They were told Constantinople wanted Alexis, but it turned out that Alexis

III had set the people against him by warning them it was all a plot to bring them under the Latins; and so they had been obliged to resort to arms to effect their purpose. Still everything had turned out well. Providence was on their side and Alexis would lead them to Palestine.

Innocent was not deceived by the professions of seeking reunion of the churches. To Boniface he expressed his dissatisfaction at this second attack on a Christian people when they had only recently been absolved for the attack on Zara. If there was any real devotion to the Roman Church in the proceeding at Constantinople the offence was mitigated, but there must be repentance, for otherwise, unclean of heart, they could not set out whole-heartedly to recover the Holy Land.

Meanwhile, in Constantinople, and entirely unknown to Innocent, violence followed violence with increasing savagery so that not till the spring of 1204 was order re-established and the new Latin kingdom set up.

From the first, Alexis IV was a failure as emperor. The city soon hated him because in his want of money he devised impossible schemes of taxation, endeavouring by any means however disreputable to get funds for the army of crusaders whom he had promised to pay lavishly for bringing him to Constantinople.

The clergy were hostile because Alexis IV swore he would bring them under the obedience of Rome. The crusaders, their pay heavily in arrears, lingered hard by the city waiting for the money that was to come to them. Every week things got more hopeless for Alexis IV and his father and fellow emperor Isaac. Their brief rule crashed when a general uprising, led by one Murzuphlus, swept them out of power and left Alexis IV strangled. Murzuphlus—Alexis V—would have come to terms with the crusaders but for his rooted objection to the supremacy of the pope over the Greek bishops. While he stood out the leaders of the crusade decided on action.

Constantinople must be taken, as Zara had been taken, and a Latin emperor chosen to rule over it.

Sack of Constantinople

The army, penniless, was reconciled to such an assault by an assurance that the indulgence the Church promised them, would be earned by the capture of the city as certainly as by attacking the Saracens. Boniface, indifferent to Innocent's commands, satisfied that the pope would not know, and therefore could not interfere till it was all over, gave the word for the assault. Constantinople fell before the crusading army. The "new Rome" of the empire, with its Christian tradition that dated from the conversion of Constantine, its wealth accumulated through nine long centuries, its churches and convents enriched with treasure beyond price, was the spoil of an army wanting its pay and grown impatient with waiting.

Murzuphlus made his escape before the onslaught. Boniface and his captains decided that Baldwin, count of Flanders, should be emperor, while Dandalo and the Venetians claimed the right to appoint the patriarch. Boniface, compensated with territories on the European side of the Bosphorus, took Salonika.

The army rushed on its prey. Fire and sword, pent up passions and lusts of a disciplined soldiery ("pilgrims" who had taken the cross in the service of Christianity!) released, murder and theft unhindered, made the sack of Constantinople by the crusaders on those days of early April, a.d. 1204, an appalling and shocking event in the stained annals of the crusades. The horrors were unspeakable. They were "schismatics," these Greek Christians — that was justification enough for robbing their churches, violating their nuns, killing all who resisted. So the crusaders argued—if any argument was necessary for sacking Constantinople.

It is, of course, true that in the past jealousy and fear of Rome had over and over again persuaded emperor and patriarch of Constantinople to frustrate as far as possible the efforts of the crusaders to recover the Holy Land from the Moslems. Latins and Venetians resident in Constantinople had suffered under the oppressive rule of the Greeks. But this capture of the city was no part of the plan of the fourth crusade; neither was it contemplated at the outset by its leaders. Wholly repugnant to the mind of Innocent III was forcible annexation. The statesmanship of Innocent, directed to the welfare of Europe, counted for nothing when the commerce of Venice and the ambitions of French nobles were concerned. Constantinople a shambles, looted to the uttermost, Baldwin, count of Flanders, was proclaimed first Latin emperor of the East; Venetian canons installed in St. Sophia chose a Venetian, Tommaso Morosini, for their patriarch.

The work accomplished, Tommaso with envoys from Baldwin and Dandalo set out for Rome that the pope might bless their conquests. Had they not ended the "schism" and brought Constantinople within the bosom of Rome?

Innocent, long kept in ignorance of what had happened at Constantinople, learning only from reports that reached him far later of the sack of the city, was astonished and delighted when the letter came from Baldwin, an enthusiastic and extremely plausible letter, full of highly coloured phrases of the good work done by the crusaders in bringing Constantinople under the obedience of the pope. There had been fighting, of course, Baldwin explained, for Alexis IV had behaved like the perfidious Greek he was, and another Greek, Murzuphlus, after killing Alexis had attacked them. Now the Greek rule in Constantinople was finished. The wretched Greeks, always enemies of Rome, haters of Latin people—refusing to allow images to be made of Christ, our Lord—were punished by the Latins they had abused. Henceforth the way was open for the crusaders to the Holy Land. The writer, now emperor of the East—emperor of Romania—would depart to Palestine directly he had reestablished order in his new dominions. Both for the honour of the holy Roman Church and for the profit of the Holy Land had Constantinople been taken. All that was wanted was that the pope should summon a general council to meet in Constantinople, preside over it in person and send priests and monks to reconcile the inhabitants to the Latin rite. It would also be a good thing to get people from Italy settled in the Eastern empire in order to defend it from enemies. Meantime they all waited expectantly for the papal blessing on what had been done.

Similar letters came from Boniface and other leaders. Letters calculated to move Innocent to thankfulness that God had wrought such wonders. Disillusionment, bitter disillusionment, would come when, with fuller information, the truth was known. For the moment Innocent could only rejoice that the East was restored to union with the West. Not a hint came from the Latin conquerors of Constantinople that the Greek clergy were even more than ever disaffected from Rome.

Innocent's reply to the new emperor of Constantinople expressed the happiness of the pope at the startling news. Let the crusaders henceforth protect the empire of the East and by that means free the Holy Land from pagans. It was for the emperor, whom the pope now took under his care, to bring all the Greek empire within the spiritual obedience of the holy Roman Church, and to guard carefully all ecclesiastical property, so that the things of Caesar should be rendered to Caesar and the things of God to God. At the same time the election of Tommaso to the patriarchate was quite irregular. It was not for the emperor to make such an appointment; as for the Venetian canons who had chosen Tommaso, they had not been properly instituted as canons. However, for once Innocent would overlook these irregularities, and, since the emperor wished for Tommaso, Tommaso Morosini should be appointed. Yet it must not by any means be taken for a precedent. In future when a bishopric was vacant all elections must take place according to canon law. Innocent himself then consecrated Tommaso as bishop and patriarch of Constantinople. That was on mid-lent Sunday, in 1205. Innocent was already uneasy on hearing that his legate, Cardinal Peter, after concluding a six years' truce with the Saracens in Palestine, had gone to Constantinople without consulting the pope.

Gradually, now from one source, now from another, but more particularly from the mouths of entirely trustworthy and first-hand witnesses, Innocent learnt the real truth concerning the "deeds of darkness" at the taking of Constantinople. To Cardinal Peter he wrote in burning indignation, for his papal legate had already absolved from their vows as crusaders men who had stayed more than a year in Constantinople, men who, as the pope pointed out, were but thinking of temporal gain. These men had brought the crusade to ignoble failure, destroying all hope of success. Innocent went on to write with customary use of biblical texts of the dreadful atrocities committed by the crusaders, crimes that made it impossible for the Christians of the Greek Church to desire unity with the see of Rome. After what had taken place the Greeks would loathe the Latins worse than dogs and not unjustly would they loathe them. Had not these Latin crusaders covered themselves with the blood of Christians, respecting neither religion, nor age, nor sex in their wickedness ? Had they not violated holy virgins consecrated to God, had they not robbed and murdered rich and poor, and plundered the very altars in the churches?

To Boniface, the captain and commander of the crusading army, Innocent wrote with no less severity. The count of Montferrat had neither jurisdiction nor authority over the Greeks whom he had conquered; he had sullied the vows the crusader, turning his arms against Christians instead of against the Saracens, and coveting earthly treasure rather than heavenly, had taken Constantinople, leaving Jerusalem undelivered. Again Innocent recounted with terrible emphasis the crimes committed at the taking of the city. But since wrongs done could not be undone, let Boniface rule the land in justice, return to the Church all stolen property, make atonement for the sins committed, and once more take up the cause of the Holy Land. The conquest of Constantinople might yet be of help to the recovery of Jerusalem.

Innocent's hopes flickered, dwindled, and were swiftly extinguished. The fourth crusade was a lost cause when Baldwin, count of Flanders, reigned as emperor of the East, Once more the pope recognised the facts. He and he alone, it may be said, realised the danger to Christendom from the coming power of the Saracens, noting the threat to the small part of Palestine left in Christian hands, pointing out that with all Palestine lost the empire of Constantinople would eventually be reconquered by the Greeks. Baldwin's glorious program of an advance from Constantinople to the Holy Land would never be carried out; the vows of the Crusaders never fulfilled. On the contrary it became evident to Innocent that Constantinople would draw men away from the Holy Land rather than send them there, would itself need help from Europe if the Latin kingdom was to be maintained.

Before all was lost in Palestine, and while the six years truce with the Saracens endured, Innocent made several tempts to revive an interest in the crusades. Philip of France was not to be moved, but it was a Frenchman, John of Brienne, that same John of Brienne once employed in the war in Sicily, and now titular king of Jerusalem, who was prepared to make a stand if supported. The support from Europe was not given. The fourth crusade disappointed all the hopes of Innocent; yet he continued to warn Christendom against being lulled into false notions of security. The Moslem power threatened Europe and would continue to threaten Europe unless Christian princes armed and did battle for the cross. Let men be enrolled for a three-year war, let the Christian ports provide ships. A fifth crusade was preached as before, but no longer now could military knights earn the indulgence by fighting against Albigensian heretics in Provence, against Moors in Spain; henceforth all must depart to the East to be accounted true crusaders. Innocent called on Europe to arm while yet he laboured for peace, writing to Saladin's brother an earnest appeal to let the Christians have Jerusalem and thereby put an end to all further bloodshed. No profit but much loss would come to the Saracens by holding Jerusalem, why not let it be given to the Christians? The appeal was very coldly received. It convinced the Moslems that Rome was now their enemy, its pope the directing energy of the crusades. The religion of Islam encouraged no surrender of conquests for the sake of peace.

Innocent did not live to see the fifth crusade. Yet more than any other man was he responsible for the enterprise. The Lateran Council of 1215 that Innocent assembled concerned itself with the crusade and decided on the time and place of its departure. To the last he stood out against the Turks, believing that by the preservation of the Holy Land from Turkish rule the Christendom of Europe was safeguarded.

The Children's Crusade

Gross elements of worldly ambition, lust of power, love of money—elements conspicuous in human affairs throughout the ages—discolour the history of the crusades, largely concealing the finer qualities that, after all, were never completely absent. Many a knight in England and France left home and family to die in Palestine, killed in battle or wasted in captivity, looking for no reward on earth, stirred to battle for the honour of His Lord, excited to action by thought of the holy places, Jerusalem in especial, in the hands of the enemies of the cross of Christ. Likely to be overlooked are the single-minded, unself-conscious knights of the crusades who responded to the appeals of Innocent, counting the world well lost for the high adventure to which they were called. Restless no doubt, for the times were restless, as Richard, king of England, Richard of the Lion-heart was restless. Moved by sheer devotion to the common Lord and Saviour of all Christians were others, as St. Louis, king of France was moved. Disinterested they appeared to contemporaries, their motives appreciated by thousands, themselves unwilling to pursue exalted ideals. Holiness was recognised in the Middle Ages, sanctity reverenced by multitudes living graceless lives. So it was in the crusades. So it was particularly in the case of that most pathetic, most astounding event—the children's crusade of 1212.

One totally unexpected result of the preaching of the crusade in France was the departure of children, many thousands of children by all accounts—but round numbers must always be accepted with reserve and, where no statistics are available exaggeration haunts compilers of figures—from the province of Orleans and from the Rhineland. A shepherd boy named Stephen, who came from Troyes, started the idea of children rescuing Jerusalem, and his fervent exhortation brought young people from all the neighbouring villages to listen to the tale he told. The enthusiasm spread and another youth, Nicholas, took up the story in his village near Cologne.

As the Pied Piper of Hamlin drew the children after him by his playing, so the children were drawn by Stephen and Nicholas to go marching off and would not be kept back. The clergy regarded the exodus without approval. Parents could only look on with amazement at the spectacle, helpless it seemed to counteract the call, powerless to restrain; not knowing what it meant, fearing to hinder what perhaps was of divine inspiration. Whole villages were emptied of children.

Thousands must have perished on the way but a crowd led by Nicholas did actually cross the Alps into Italy and a remnant finally reached Brindisi; there to be sold as slaves to the highest bidder.

Nor did Stephen's French contingent fare any better, though their overland journey was shorter. For at Marseilles the children, given accommodation on two ships, merchant vessels about to sail to Palestine, embarked and were no more seen or heard of. Not till years afterwards was it learnt that these children, children of the Franks, had been sold in the slave markets of Alexandria and Baghdad.

Report of this strange, forlorn pilgrimage reached Pope Innocent and he endeavoured to stop it; apparently with but little success. But Innocent could not refrain from speaking of the example given—"the very children shame us, for they rush to the recovery of the Holy Land while we sleep."

They passed into slavery, into the bondage of the Moslem, these children of the crusade, betrayed by Christian dealers. The incident was closed. Unforeseen, unrepeated, it was the most extraordinary and most pathetic incident, this irrational project of the children's crusade, in the whole series of wars for the recovery of the Holy Land.

CHAPTER VII
The Latin Empire of the East

NO STABLE FOUNDATION—INNOCENT'S CONCILIATORY POLICY—WAR WITH BULGARIANS—DEATH OF BALDWIN—FEUDS OF FRANKS AND VENETIANS.

ROMANIA, the Latin empire of the East, was built on no stable foundation. Massacre and plunder marked the taking of Constantinople, pride and avarice thwarted continually the efforts of Pope Innocent to promote peace and good will, to establish in justice the new dynasty of the Franks. The Greeks simply would not be reconciled to the overlordship of foreigners, Venetians, whom they hated, Franks, whom they mistrusted. Resistance was stiffened by Greek clergy, as hostile as ever to the supremacy of Rome over the Church of Constantinople.

The policy of Innocent was conciliation. It was the policy he enjoined on his legates at Constantinople, on the patriarch Tommaso, on the Latin emperors. Let them above all, repeatedly he wrote, treat fairly clergy and laity brought up in the Eastern Church. Let the rites of the Greek Church be maintained, and the boundaries of bishoprics preserved. Innocent laboured in vain. Too deep seated was the hostility to the West, too contemptuous the attitude of the Franks to the "perfidious" Greeks. Neither the Balkan rulers nor their subjects were addicted to the paths of peace, much preferring chronic warfare. Constantinople itself was rent by the feuds of French and Venetians. Beyond the Bosphorous two new empires of the East were set up, and at Trebizond on the Black Sea and at Nicea—in the latter city Lascaris, son- in-law of Alexis III, became ruler—fugitives from Constantinople gathered round their chiefs. To Asia Minor went also Greek bishops who would not suffer a Latin to rule over them. The Asiatic dominion of Constantinople, which extended over comparatively small territories, Baldwin's brother Henry governed as regent.

Few and short were the days of Baldwin on the throne of the Latin empire. Jonitza, king of Bulgaria, whom Innocent had blessed and supported, cheerfully acknowledged Baldwin as a fellow sovereign, only to be met stiffly with the reply that Bulgaria was subject to Constantinople. At this rebuff—had not Bulgaria won its independence bravely, gloriously, of the Greek emperors?— Jonitza flew to arms in defence of his title. The disaffected Greeks inflamed the wounded feelings of the Bulgarian king, urging Jonitza on to war. Baldwin, hopelessly outnumbered, stood with his knights in battle array rather than admit Jonitza's claim to equal sovereignty. At Adrianople the Franks were routed and Baldwin, ever a fighter, was taken prisoner and led away to die in captivity. On the news of this disaster Henry returned from Asia Minor to be proclaimed regent, and shortly after, on the presumption of Baldwin's death, emperor. Henry wrote promptly to Innocent, denouncing the Greeks for their perfidy and treachery, denouncing Jonitza, alleging that the Bulgarian king was allied with the Turks and other enemies of the cross, imploring the pope, "their father and their lord," the "only refuge and foundation of our hopes" to bring them help from the west to the new empire. In the common opinion of the Christians in the East, Henry added, the liberation of the Holy Land no less than the unity of the Church depended on the existence of the Latin empire. Both the

Templars and the Hospitallers on this were agreed. (But the dissident Greeks were certainly not of this opinion.)

Innocent at once answered the appeal, bidding Henry make peace with Jonitza "our greatly beloved son, king of the Bulgarians." At the same time Innocent sent word to crusaders in Europe and in Palestine to rally to the defence of the Latin empire for the sake of Jerusalem. Innocent next wrote to Jonitza, reminding him of the crown he had sent him, bidding him make peace with Constantinople before trouble fell upon him from the armies of Europe then on their march to the East.

Jonitza replied that he would give his very head for the pope. But really the Latins had behaved badly, treating his honourable peace proposals with contempt on their capture of Constantinople. With the sacred banner of St. Peter which he received from Rome itself had he fought against these false crusaders.

Another letter went from Henry to the pope "the father of all and in especial our father" mentioning fresh troubles—the Bulgarians had again been victorious over the Latins. On this Pope Innocent persuaded a body of crusaders to divert their course to Constantinople and again appealed to Jonitza to make peace.

However, in that year 1206 occurred the murder of Jonitza and a poor creature, one Boris of Boril, succeeded the stalwart fighting man as king of Bulgaria. But Boris had a daughter whose beauty was much extolled by all who saw her. Henry married the beautiful daughter of King Boris and thereby ended all war with the Bulgarians. The Latin empire of the East by this marriage was now safe enough on its northern frontiers, but Henry, a far more capable ruler than Baldwin, had trouble enough from enemies, within the empire and from without, till death came to him ten years later. His relations with Innocent were cordial throughout his reign. Henry knew how much he relied on the help of the pope, Innocent counted on the emperor at Constantinople to maintain the Catholic cause in the East.

French feudalism was incompatible with the civilisation—such as it was—of the Greeks. This incompatibility meant constant friction between the Frankish conquerors and the native population; it brought dissolution of the old existing forms of civil government. Inevitably forms of government, civil and ecclesiastical alike, were held of small account by knights and lesser nobles from the West, sheer adventurers for the most part, now set up as rulers, knowing nothing of the Greeks, owing nothing but feudal service to the emperor. All Greece and the Morea and many islands of the Archipelago were included in this "new France" of the Latin empire of the East. The feudal system with its castles, its military methods, its utter disregard of foreign social customs and political institutions long prevalent, its general indifference to the observances of religion, was naturally seen as something hostile and alien by the Greeks, whose bishops, retreating-before the Frankish invaders and settling in Asia, simply declined all intercourse with the intruders. Nor did the clergy who accompanied the feudal lords improve the relations of Greeks and Latins. In the eyes of Pope Innocent too many of these clerics appeared as self- seekers, men eager for personal gain rather than the good estate of the Christian Church.

The Latin empire of the East was always a source of anxiety to Innocent, but nothing shook the pope's confident assurance that while Constantinople was held by Latins of the West the way of the Turk was obstructed, the passage to Europe barred against the forces of Islam. "Romania" was demanded by statesmanship for the sake of Christendom. In spite of the present difficulties it was still an opening for the recovery of the Holy Land, for the return of the Greek churches to the unity of the Roman Church. Over and over again the letters of Pope Innocent dwell on these topics, repeat the same arguments, varying the biblical quotations. Feudal lords paid little heed, Byzantine bishops would not budge from their stiffness. Ecclesiastical proceedings in Constantinople, even with the city subject to Rome, did not invite the Greek episcopate to reunion. In the Constantinople they had so substantially helped to conquer, the Venetians saw a Venetian colony. The Church of Constantinople, consequently, no longer Greek must be Venetian. Tommaso the patriarch, having been safely exalted to the archbishop's throne by the Venetian canons in possession of St. Sophia, it was for Tommaso to see that his successors would be chosen by Venetians. Hence Tommaso, calling at Venice on his way back from Rome to Constantinople, was persuaded (or coerced, for the newly consecrated patriarch was owing money to Venetians) to take an oath that he would appoint none but Venetians to the canonries of St. Sophia and in every way do his best to keep the patriarchate in Venetian hands, in all Romania making no bishops except Venetians.

Innocent, when he came to hear of it, of course, at once quashed this entirely irregular oath. But he could not induce the French clergy to hold their Venetian patriarch in esteem; for a while in their indignation they refused him all respect, all obedience. This recalcitrancy the Franks held to be justifiable, alleging the election of Tommaso to be a corrupt and dishonest transaction. What rankled was the open and evident fact that by some means or another the Venetians, having got the better of the French in the distribution of important church appointments, were endeavouring to keep these appointments in their hands forever. The new papal legate, Cardinal Benedict, a wise and sensible prelate in the eyes of his contemporaries, made peace between the patriarch and his refractory clergy, while Innocent did what he could to support the authority of Tommaso, an authority flouted by all the non-Venetian groups in Constantinople.

Tommaso Morosini was not exactly an exemplary patriarch though his personal and private life incurred no reproach. Charges and counter-charges of financial illegalities, of irregularities in episcopal appointments brought repeated appeals to Rome. When he died Tommaso was under orders from the pope to pay back certain sums of money due to the clergy if the commissioners sent from Rome were satisfied that the money was justly owing.

No sooner was the patriarchate vacant than Venetians and Franks prepared for a fiercely contested election. Venetians meant to retain the archbishop's throne, with all the wealth and patronage that belonged to the patriarch; the Franks were resolved to put up a fight for it. They were irked by having a Venetian for their spiritual head. The Venetians won on election day, for they filled the cathedral with armed men ready to kill or wound all electors on the opposite side, and then left the canons, or at least a certain number of them, to choose their dean as patriarch. The heads of the various religious houses specially named as electors by Innocent were thus disfranchised. Thereupon the Franks appealed to Rome against this scandalous and uncanonical election and proposed to the pope a choice of three names of their own selection.

Innocent declared the election null and void—as it too obviously was—and ordered a fresh election; with no better result. For each side claimed that their man had been elected. The only way out of the deadlock, since the factions would not come to terms, was to administer the patriarchate from Rome and the papal legate, Pelagius, a Portuguese cardinal, was sent as administrator with instructions to do what he could to bring this scandalous clerical feud of Venetians and French to an end. It went on for years, this feud, till at the great Lateran Council of 1215 the nominees of both parties presented themselves to urge their respective claims. Then Innocent settled the matter by setting both candidates aside and appointing a Tuscan priest, Gervase, to the patriarchate.

The wretched division of French and Venetians brought no persuasion to the Greeks that reunion with Rome was essential to salvation; such reunion did not appear even desirable. The arbitrary conduct of the legate Pelagius made matters worse. The Emperor Henry treated the Greeks in kindly fashion, his justice was never impugned. But Pelagius, as papal legate, would have all the clergy acknowledge the pope as head of the Church and met the passive resistance of the Greeks by inaugurating a reign of violence and terror. Death was threatened by the legate to priests who left the name of the pope out of service books; many of these priests were imprisoned in chains, many Greek monks thrown into prison; the churches of the Greeks were closed. Only after a piteous appeal to the emperor was the legate's decree annulled. In opposition to the commands of Pelagius, Henry ordered the churches to be re-opened, all monks and priests to be set free from prison. But by that time a considerable number of Greek clergy had escaped from the persecution of Constantinople to the Emperor Lascaris at Nicea. As a step towards the reunion of the Greek church with the Latin the taking of Constantinople led nowhere: the setting up of a Latin kingdom aroused animosity in the East; the proceedings of the Catholics of the West within the kingdom provoked resentment and produced not the peace that Innocent desired, but bitter and lasting hatred.

They defeated his plans, Innocent's professed subjects in the Latin empire, making a mock of Christian charity and good will, trampling under foot the law of justice that Innocent would have extended to the Greeks.

Yet till the end of his days Innocent never wavered in his support of the Emperor Henry; nor was the pope's conviction shaken that Constantinople held by the West was a bulwark against the Turkish invasion of Europe. Till the end of his days

Innocent also looked for a recovery of the Holy Land and a reconciliation with the eastern churches separated from the Apostolic See. The Latin empire of the East was to last for more than fifty years; but for Innocent III it would hardly have endured for five.

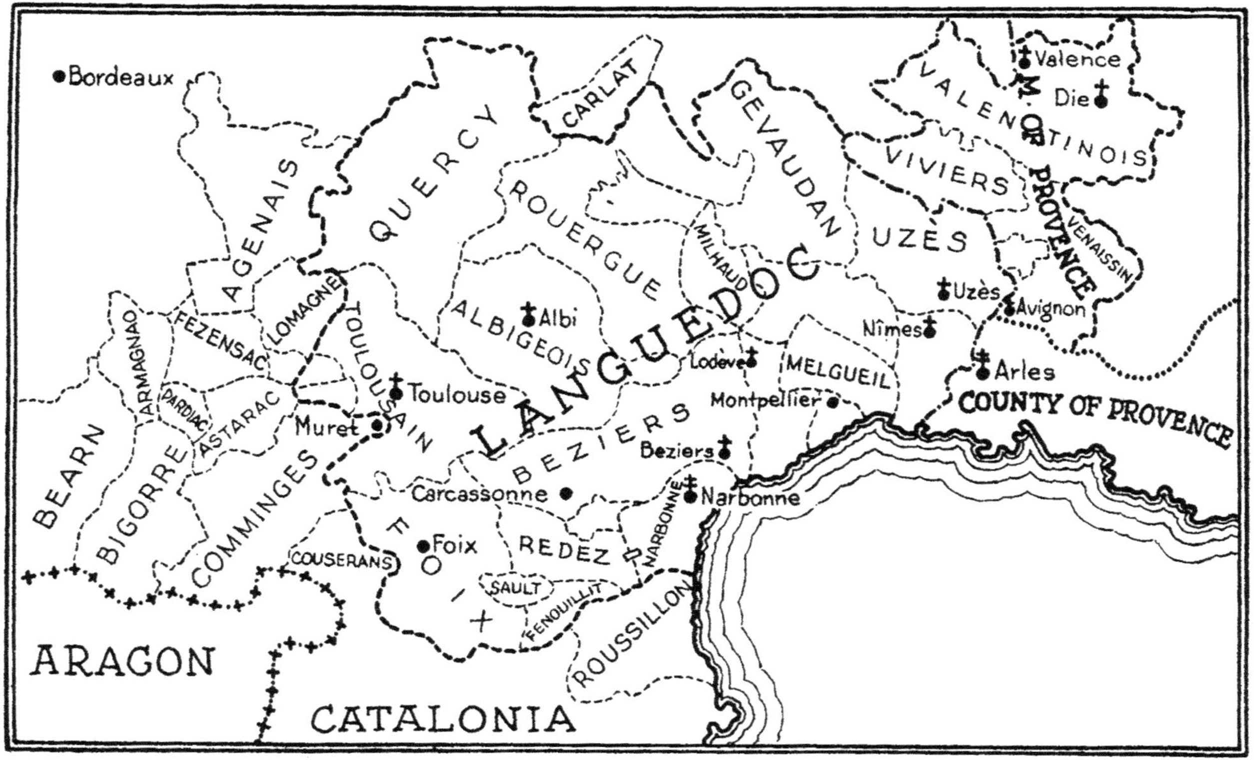

Bordeaux
AGENAIS
QUERCY
CARLAT
ROUERGUE
GEVAUDAN
VALENTINOIS
M. OF PROVENCE
Valence
Die
VIVIERS
UZÈS
VENAISSIN
Uzès
Avignon
Nîmes
Arles
COUNTY OF PROVENCE
MILHAUD
LANGUEDOC
ALBIGEOIS
Albi
Lodève
MELGUEIL
Montpellier
LOMAGNE
FEZENSAC
ARMAGNAC
PARDIAC
ASTARAC
TOULOUSAIN
Toulouse
Muret
BEARN
BIGORRE
COMMINGES
BEZIERS
Beziers
Narbonne
Carcassonne
FOIX
Foix
REDEZ
NARBONNE
COUSERANS
SAULT
FENOUILLIT
ROUSSILLON
ARAGON
CATALONIA

CHAPTER VIII
Albigensian and Other Heresies in the West

Nature of Catharist or Albigensian Dogma—Its Wide Acceptance in Southern France—Support of Count Raymond VI of Toulouse—Innocent's Missionaries—Arrival of Dominic and Bishop Diego—Murder of Papal Legate—Crusade Against the Albigenses—Overthrow at Battle of Muret—Franciscan Antidote to Waldensian Heresy—Abbot Joachim of Flora.

WHO can say when the missionaries of Catharist[17] heresy first settled in the rich lands of Languedoc and Provence? A hundred years before the pontificate of Innocent III heresy was taking root in the southeast of France, finding adherents in Milan, spreading in Italy. Condemned by numerous Church Councils throughout the twelfth century—notably at Toulouse and Tours and the Lateran—preached against by St. Bernard, it grew and flourished till all the highly cultured province of Languedoc was predominantly Catharist, town and county of Toulouse

---

[17] From the Greek word *katharos*, i.e., the morally pure.

openly adopting this anti-Catholic, anti-Christian religion in preference to the faith of the holy Roman Church. Since Albi was a centre and stronghold of the heresy, "Albigensian" became the general title of the various groups, fundamentally in agreement that matter was evil in itself, that the pope was the enemy to be destroyed.

Nature of Catharist Dogma

From the East came this doctrine of the twin forces of good and evil, St. Augustine in youth had fallen under its sway, knowing it as Manichean. Manichean it remained while its disciples carried the teaching from the Paulician church of Armenia in Asia Minor to Thrace and the Balkan lands; thence north to Hungary, westwards to France and Lombardy. Bulgarians or Bogomiles, in Italy Patarines, in France Catharists or Albigenses, whatever the minor differences of the sects, the doctrine is common. Indeed it is impossible to explain the niceties that distinguished one group of these sectaries from another. (In Lombardy in the twelfth century the leaders of seven different sects are reported to have met for public disputation, while in Milan alone seventeen different sects, it was alleged, rejoiced in separate congregations.) No definite Albigensian statement of belief has been preserved. We depend on the evidence of converts and contemporary opponents for our knowledge. It is sufficient, this evidence, for a fairly clear view of the Albigensian dogma and its social ethics. Why this exotic doctrine should have made such a successful appeal to the inhabitants of Provence is not to be so clearly seen, unless its social ethics—and a general ignorance of Christianity—are considered.

The problems of the existence of evil in a world created and governed by God, omnipotent and good, perplexes many souls to-day. It perplexed many in the Middle Ages. The Albigensian dogma offered a solution. Not one God but two was the explanation. What we may call the purely spiritual was, according to the Albigensian, alone the work of the good God; all that is material, including the human body, was the work of the evil power. Between them, God and the devil ruled the world. The business of the true Albigensian believer was to spurn utterly the body and all its works.

Such a dogma naturally involved complete denial of the Christian faith in the Incarnation of Christ and our redemption through His death and resurrection. Christ to the Albigensian was but a spirit, for a while appearing in human form, but only *appearing;* since this human form was not real, the crucifixion of this ghostly being but an illusion. The New Testament read by the Albigensian—New Testament readings having been a feature of the meetings of these people—revealed a purely spiritual Christ who preached the Albigensian doctrine and taught that in every man the soul held a spark of the divine essence that could be trained to overcome the evil of the body and thus achieve everlasting salvation. Whilever the soul was imprisoned in the body it was in danger of final damnation; and there was only one way of defeating the devil and that was by taking the *Consolamentum,* a simple enough rite in itself but involving the most tremendous consequences on the recipient. To take the *Consolamentum* was to join the ranks of the Perfect (or Perfected) the ruling elders of the Albigensian church, and to follow a life of extreme abstinence; the body to be starved by long fasting and vowed to chastity. As far as public life was concerned the Perfect refused all oaths and engagements in lawsuits.

Under the circumstances the average Albigensian naturally kept away from the *Consolamentum,* postponing till his deathbed, when all chance of recovery was remote, this reception into the company of the Perfect, with its assurance of salvation. He was not required as a true Albigensian to do more than promise to take the *Consolamentum* and hold the Perfect in reverence. The alarming thing was the return of health to the patient when given up as incurable, he had taken the *Consolamentum.* For now must he live the mortified existence of the Perfect cut off from the bodily pleasures of eating and drinking—often so peculiarly grateful to the convalescent—doomed to the meagrest, dullest diet, denied all return to sex relations. It was a prospect that frightened the stoutest hearts so that the alternative—suicide—was preferred. The form of suicide known as *Endura* was starvation (hunger striking it is called in our times), and the Perfect saw to it that no food reached the dying man. Fortunately few recovered to face the dread alternatives; so far as we know.

Pope Innocent confronted with the challenge of the Catharists in Provence recognised the gravity of the issue; discerned the *why* and the *how* of the success of the Albigensians. Here was no obscure sect of Christian men led into error through misunderstanding. The Catharists were heretics in the right sense of that often ill-used word. Insisting that they and they alone had the truth, the Catholic Church was opposed by them as the enemy of enlightenment, its pope denounced as the harlot of the seven hills of Rome mentioned in the Apocalypse of St. John.[18] No room existed for Catholics and Catharists in the same land. One or the other must go down in the struggle between the two. The Catharists, strongly entrenched, numerically increasing, commercially prosperous, socially respected, held the conviction that Catholic Christianity was the lost cause. To all appearances in Languedoc the conviction was not unreasonable.

Ignorance, sheer ignorance of the Christian religion and the Catholic faith was the opportunity of the Catharist

---

[18] Probably the anti-papal invective has encouraged various Protestant writers to treat the Albigensians as forerunners of the Reformation. An examination of the Catharist doctrine would soon dispel that notion.

missionaries; they made full use of it. Parish priests gave no instruction to their flocks, were indeed quite unable to preach, incompetent to expound the Gospel of Christ. An ignorant and illiterate clergy could but leave an ignorant laity at the mercy of any fantastic creed vigorously advocated. Conditions in Languedoc were more than elsewhere in France favourable to the heretics. The episcopate was deplorable. Bishops and archbishops, feudal nobles chosen by cathedral chapters composed of lesser nobles, patronised the Catharists; in some cases openly favoured them; in general wished to stand well with men so obviously powerful—to avoid trouble. An illiterate priesthood could hardly do other than follow the lead of its bishops. The laity could join the heretics without fear of reproof. By Innocent's time not to be a Catharist—in Toulouse for instance—was to be excluded from all the privileges of the established religion; to stand no chance of doing well in business; to be, in short, outside all civic life.

Nothing effective could be done to check the spread of Catharist heresy, to prevent its consolidation, to hinder its growth or discredit its reputation, while the Catholic hierarchy lived in luxurious disorder and the lay nobility kept on friendly and intimate terms with the Catharist leaders.

The ostentatious pride and wealth of the archbishops, their indifference to Christian morality—they lived openly with concubines, made war with hired troops on their neighbours, and extracted heavy fees from clergy nominated to bishoprics, from laity seeking dispensations—contrasted with the way of life of the Perfect and struck god-fearing men as the fruits of a radically defective doctrine. Catholic Christianity produced, inevitably produced, these corrupt prelates who so freely indulged their gross carnal appetites—so they judged, these plain men and women of town and country in Languedoc. Time had inured the population to the habits and customs of clergy singularly unfitted to be examples of Christian life; it made them the more readily accept and retain the Catharist teaching. The Perfect of the Albigensian church did actually live the ascetism they preached. No charge of hypocrisy or humbug is recorded. They were in deadly earnest bent on the overthrow of a Catholic Christianity held to be based on falsehood.

Innocent's immediate predecessors in the papacy, old men exhausted in their struggles with the empire, could do nothing to keep back the invasive tide of heresy. Neither argument nor force were available. The Catharist leaders knew their case, and could state it. Who among the Catholics in southern France could dispute in public with the Catharists, refute their arguments and get the better of their logic? Once firmly established in Languedoc, recognisably powerful and influential in all classes of society, the Albigensians challenged the Catholic Christianity of Europe, and the challenge was not taken up.

But Innocent III was not the man to decline such a challenge, to allow so fair a part of France to be lost to Christendom. He sent his legates everywhere and for the most part was well served by the clerics wisely chosen for the work. (Peter the legate in Palestine and Pelagius at Constantinople proved less suitable than might have been expected.) From his legate in Provence Innocent learnt of the existing conditions in a number of dioceses, of the character of the bishops, and of the attitude of Raymond VI, count of Toulouse, duke of Narbonne, marquis of Provence, whose father, Raymond V, fully alive to the danger of Albigensian heresy vainly sought to counteract it by imploring the help of the Cistercian monks. (These were immensely wealthy, but at least their monasteries were of good repute, free from the scandals that disfigured monastic life in southern France.)

On Innocent's accession the Albigensians were at their strongest. Commercially Languedoc flourished under the heretics. Prosperity attended, naturally attended, a people discouraged from taking pleasure where they found it, exhorted to seriousness and a life of industry. Joy was not to be had, according to the Albigensian doctrine, in the happiness of family life, in social fellowship with its eating and drinking—all bodily pleasures were vanity and worse since the body was the enemy of the soul. By strict attention to business, by following closely his trade and calling, the plain man could best direct his energies to his latter end, to the total annihilation of the body and its desires. And this concentration on business, on the hard work of farm and homestead, on the trade of weaving—the weaver is conspicuous in the annals of Albigensian Languedoc—did, of course, bring its reward. It always does in every age and every land. Absorbed in the pursuit of money, taught to despise both the spiritual interests of the Christian religion and the physical delights possible to average humanity, labouring people and the middle class went their respective ways with passions atrophied, strongly attached to the Albigensian church.

On the other hand, while it proposed a narrow but successful existence to the hard-working, serious-minded people, this Albigensianism appealed no less strongly, perhaps even more strongly, to knights and nobles, to the troubadours, to the ladies of rank and fashion, to the wealthy cultivated descendants of Moors and Jews long settled in Provence. A rich civilisation, with its langour and moral corruption, had no hostility to a religion that left men and women free to indulge all libidinous desires, requiring only a death-bed renunciation of the pleasures of life. The Albigensian teaching concerning marriage was quite agreeable to the sensual man.

It is not to be believed that the serious, industrious Albigensian refrained from marriage and the begetting of children. The heresy would have died a natural death had the population dwindled. The Perfect discountenanced marriage; they did not prohibit, they could not prohibit the natural union of the male and female. By decrying the Christian doctrine of marriage, denying the sacramental character of holy matrimony, refusing to discriminate between monogamy and polygamy—since all bodily indulgence was evil why discriminate between taking many wives or one?—the Perfect removed reproach from adultery and promiscuous fornication. Love, romantic love, became the theme of poets and troubadours, and it was something quite different from the love of husband and wife, of parent and child. Romantic love was not hampered by sense of responsibility, it acknowledged no bonds, the mistress extolled by troubadour poets and singers was as likely as not to be another man's wife as a simple maid. It was all one to the poet of Provence. Romantic love did not include the vision of life-long union; neither did it contemplate so prosaic an affair as setting up a home, nor allow any virtue in the happiness of family life. Romantic love suited the sensualist and was not condemned by the asceticism of the Perfect. Sensualist and ascetic in Provence spurning the Christian ethic of marriage despised the fidelity it enjoined on husband and wife.[19]

Support of Count Raymond VI of Toulouse

Count Raymond VI of Toulouse, whose matrimonial ventures and divorces are beyond enumeration, was drawn irresistibly to the Catharists. Archbishops and bishops of

---

[19] Echoes may be heard of this twelfth-century song of romantic love in later ages; we have heard it extolled even in our own times to the disparagement of Christian marriage; the latter, involving fidelity of vows solemnly professed, is dismissed as *bourgeois*. For a fuller account of the essentially anti-Christian character of the troubadour cult of romantic love in the twelfth-century Provence, consult *L'Amour et L'Occident* by Denis de Rougemont (Libraire Plon, Paris, 1939). Nineteenth-century writers, praising troubadour and romantic love, were generally quite ignorant of the relation to the Catharist heresy.

southern France preferring concubines to chastity had no quarrel with a heresy that favoured incontinency rather than marriage.

Additional reasons were found for supporting the Albigensians. To plunder the Catholic Church was praiseworthy, since as an institution it had no right to property according to the teachings of the heretics, and was the object of denunciation in the Apocalypse of St. John. Release from obligations to military service was allowed to all who professed conscientious objection to war, and the payment of taxes was condemned rather than approved by certain of the Albigensian sects that inclined to communism and anarchism.

Innocent in the first year of his pontificate appointed two legates to counteract a heresy notoriously successful in southern France. For ten years he laboured to restore Christianity to a land that so generally rejected it. Only when spiritual and intellectual forces failed did the pope fall back on coercion, resolved to save by violence what could not be won by reason.

Excellent men were the legates chosen by Innocent to confute the heretics, one of them being that Guido of Montpellier whose charity founded hospitals and organised the Brothers of the Holy Spirit. It was their mission to summon the archbishops of Languedoc and the count of Toulouse to banish the Catharist leaders and all professors of heresy. Which was precisely what neither archbishops nor Count Raymond VI would do. Berenger, archbishop of Narbonne, long addicted to the worship of mammon and personal ease; never troubled even to visit his diocese, preferring to live in comfort in the abbey of Mount Aragon, keeping the revenues of canonries and parish churches in his own hands rather than make appointments to fill the vacancies. Sternly wrote Innocent to this chief bishop of the church in Languedoc of the neglect of duties, the ignoring of papal legates and letters; reproaching him for extortion and many violations of canon law. Archbishop Berenger simply took no notice of admonitions, continuing to live as he had done in the past ten years, gathering riches—some of his money went to the support of relatives—while Catharists permeated the land and Christians dwindled. Innocent bore with this incorrigible archbishop who ignored reproof and would not be intimidated; bore with him until the long-suffering pope, seeing no hope of amendment, was compelled to pass sentence of deprivation. But it took a long time to get Berenger finally deposed from the archiepiscopal throne, so various were the legal and political obstacles that prevented execution of sentence. One by one the rest of the hierarchy of Languedoc—notably the bishops of Toulouse, deposed for simony, of Carcassonne, of Beziers—were deprived of episcopal jurisdiction, their powers handed over to the pope's legates. The letters of Innocent are full of the shameful conduct of the bishops of Languedoc. For the sake of money, he wrote, they connived at all the evils of an ignorant, ill-living clergy and allowed churches to be in the care of heretics. The monks were no better, Innocent declared; giving up their lives to money-lending and gambling, to hunting and harlotry, practising as lawyers in some cases, as medical men in others; not even disdaining the profession of jongleur, giving exhibitions as clowns. The indictment does not bring all the monasteries of Provence under condemnation. On the Cistercians Innocent relied for help in the campaign against the Albigenses. A "considerable number," is the pope's estimate of the unfrocked monks in his day who voluntarily renounced the religious life for the ways of the world.

 With the hierarchy what it was, with Raymond VI and his knights neutral, it was little the papal missionaries could do. Nothing but war against the heretics would save Languedoc from being lost to Christendom, Innocent was told; and war was the last thing Innocent would countenance. Yet sooner or later the decision had to be made. The Catharist conquest of this corner of France presumed further conquests. This formidable heresy unchecked would disintegrate the Christendom of Europe.

The preaching of that most charitable man, Guido of Montpellier and his companion, made no impression on Catholic bishops sunk in sloth, on Count Raymond and his nobles busy with petty wars, on earnest and aggressive Albigensians looking for the overthrow of Christianity. Cistercian monks, including Arnold, the abbot of the mother house at Citeaux, were joined to the papal mission when Peter of Castelnau and Raoul—themselves Cistercians—became Innocent's legates. Two Cistercian bishops, Fulk, once a troubadour and now successor of the prelate discharged for simony from the diocese of Toulouse, and the other, bishop of Auxerre—strengthened the Catholic cause. For all the zeal displayed against the Catharists, for all the sermons and instructions, and despite a vigorous controversy, the Cistercians confessed their mission a failure. Protected by Count Raymond the Catharists derided the Cistercian mission. The rank and file of the Albigensian Church remained unmoved. The papal legates would have retired from Languedoc in despair if Innocent had not constrained them to stay.

The arrival at Montpellier of two Spanish clerics, sent by Innocent, Diego, bishop of Osma, and Dominic Gusman, prior and canon of the cathedral church of Osma, whom the pope had turned from their purpose of preaching to the heathen in Russia to the more urgent needs close at hand, brought new life into the mission. Bishop Diego and St. Dominic, Dante's "hallowed wrestler," diagnosed the weakness of the Catholic cause in Provence. Pomp and ceremony attended papal legates, magnificence pertained to the proceedings of mitred abbots. All the grandeur of high ecclesiastical office bore down the orthodoxy of prelates anxious to disprove the Albigensian heresy. The people noted the simplicity and ascetism of the Albigensian leaders; coarseness of dress, long fasts, austere life of the Perfect were known to all. Comparison with the richness of apparel of Catholic dignitaries, the solemn pageantry of a papal legate's journey, the honour and reverence that surrounded the exalted estate of the pope's representative, left the people as strongly persuaded as ever that the Albigensian ministers had the true religion. Bishop Diego and St. Dominic saw that the first thing to be done was to revive the Catholic, Christian doctrine of penance, and exhibit in all humility the fruits of that doctrine. The Manichean heresy that held so much of Provence captive must be shown to be what it was—a distorted exaggerated notion of Christian teaching, its philosophy false, as false as in the time of St. Augustine. The Catholic Church fostered the ascetism, the self-denial and way of the cross that were from the beginning contained in the Gospel of Christ. But people would only believe this when the Catholic missioners were seen by all as followers of the Crucified; men who had put away the comforts and luxuries of earthly existence to follow their Lord; who had sold all they possessed for the sake of the kingdom of Christ, and for the sake of that kingdom counted the world and its goods well lost.

Yet more was needed for the conversion of Albigenses than personal self-denial on the part of Catholic missionaries. Diego and St. Dominic—the latter was canonised a.d. 1234—had immediately realised the strength of the heretics in debate. In the presentation of their case the Catholic advocates were no match for the trained leaders of their opponents. In public disputations it always appeared that the heretics had the best of the argument. With the coming of the two Spaniards from Osma, grave theologians both, began the change, a perceptible change in the area of controversy. Now for the first time throughout Languedoc the true doctrine of Christianity was explained so that all who heard it might understand. Intellectually the Catharists no longer carried the day. A population astonished when they listened to the lucid exposition of the Catholic faith grew doubtful of the superiority of Albigensianism. It seemed incredible, so a knight is reported to have said to Bishop Fulk, that such extremely effective arguments could be brought against the Catharists. It was all so novel, so strange, withal so attractive the Catholic Christianity now preached in Provence. Its appeal was to the common people. The knights and lesser nobles had no particular interest in doctrinal heresy, yet were not prepared to fall out with their Albigensian friends and relatives. Count Raymond VI of Toulouse was their feudal lord; under his protection the Albigensian church had all the privileges of an established religion. It were ill to quarrel with the official religion—true or false.

An illiterate, inarticulate clergy was impotent to convert heretics of the subtle intelligence of the Albigensian leaders. Useless they were in the face of an enemy dialectically armed at all points. The work of conversion could only be done by men of full mental equipment. Of that Dominic, then thirty-five years old, was convinced. To the life of personal mortification must be added the robust intelligence, the lively mind, the full knowledge gained by study. Learning enflamed with charity was the pressing need for the recovery of this land from heresy: an order of men and women united in a common purpose—the service of God, the knowledge of truth; an order of clergy, unfastidious in the care of their bodies, cheerfully ascetic, ready and anxious to acquire all learning available. Then on their own ground the heretics that troubled so large a part of Europe could be met, their mistaken beliefs corrected, the heathen in far-off lands received into the light. Nothing but a new religious order, an Order of Penance, as its founder named it, could accomplish this work —so Dominic saw it; so he hoped, not vainly, Pope Innocent would see it.

The Languedoc country was not to be recovered by the peaceful method of St. Dominic. Count Raymond, forever putting off repentance, now suing at Rome for pardon, now continuing his support of the Albigenses, was an irremovable obstacle to the success of the Catholic mission. To St. Dominic it was not the hearts of the people that were at fault; it was their heads. They had to be taught the truths of religion which at present were quite grossly misunderstood.

Fire and sword swept southern France. Not by the sweet reasonableness of preaching, nor by an enlightened understanding, was the Catharist heresy to be uprooted in the country of Languedoc. Ruthlessness of Catholic crusaders, years of civil war, devastation and destruction and at the end of it all—Simon of Montfort, English earl of Leicester, the recognised successor of Raymond as count of Toulouse, with the heresy exterminated and the Perfect deposed from high estate.

The germ of the Dominican order, a community of nuns living under a rule at Prouille and directed by Dominic, is visible. A handful of clergy attached to St. Dominic at Toulouse, filled with his spirit are the first of the "preaching friars." Thus Pope Innocent described them when St. Dominic, at Rome with Bishop Fulk for the great Council of the Lateran, explained his plan. The time, on the face of it, was not exactly opportune, since the council had resolved that no new orders of religion should be set up. But Pope Innocent, long aware of the character of St. Dominic, grasping immediately the scope of such an order as that outlined by Dominic, saw that the opportunity must not be lost.

Innocent's Christian statesmanship includes judgement of character, perception of time and place for action. He recognised in Dominic Gusman a man sent from God; and shared the conviction that for the saving of Christendom there must be an educated priesthood, a body of preachers trained for their work. Strange heresies disaffected the common people all too ignorant of the Catholic faith they were supposed to believe. Strange heresies were also cropping up in the universities. The *Studium,* that third power, to many an intellect a mightier power than pope or emperor, was intrigued with Arabian and Moslem metaphysics. Paris was busily discussing what was truth and what error in all this new presentation of philosophy. Innocent relied on the "preaching friars" whom Dominic would train for the work that pressed. Priests raised up to cope with university students and professors, to confute heretics in lecture rooms and public places, to preach to the common people in the streets of market towns.

Innocent had no mind but to bless the work of Dominic and bid him go forward. It signified nothing for the moment, the positive definition of a new religious order. Since Dominic himself lived according to the rule of the canons regular of St. Augustine, Innocent let his disciples adopt that rule with such emandations as might be judged convenient. Sufficient authority was provided for the time being for all that was needed. St. Dominic returned to Toulouse satisfied, as were his disciples, that the so-called Augustinian rule would serve for the basis of the order of penance. Dominic was in Rome again the following year with his new constitutions, the Augustinian rule enlarged and supplemented. Pope Innocent was dead, but his successor Honorious III gave the papal sanction and approval to this new order of clergy not attached to cathedral churches but set apart to preach the gospel to all nations. In that year, 1216, Dominic on his return to Toulouse had for the nucleus of his new order sixteen preaching friars. Bishop Fulk, the Cistercian, allotted a church. A Catholic layman presented a house for residence. The Dominican Order of Preachers was fully inaugurated.

Years before this, the murder of the papal legate, Peter de Castelnau, by directly causing the war against the heretics, destroyed the hope of peaceful conquest through preaching.

The legate was the pope's ambassador and for his death Count Raymond was held responsible. As forty years earlier the rash, ill-spoken words of Henry II of England instigated the murder of St. Thomas of Canterbury, so it was Raymond's hasty angry speech that drove one of his officers to kill the legate.

Murder of Papal Legate

Peter de Castelnau, an eminently reasonable cleric according to the contemporary verdict, went to the court of Raymond on a last attempt to bring the count of Toulouse to a better mind; to get this most disorderly prince to give up the mercenary troops so constantly employed on behalf of the heretics against Catholics. With unusual severity Pope Innocent had rebuked the count of Toulouse in the previous year, writing to him with great sternness concerning his utter want of faith; his false dealings; his recurring wars against his neighbours—"hoping to enrich yourself in war as foul birds nourish themselves on corpses"; his refusal to abstain from ravaging monastic lands even on Sundays and holydays, and not least his open patronage of the Catharists, and boast that a Catharist bishop could give better account of his faith than a Catholic bishop. Other charges are set out in this letter of Innocent's. In effect Raymond VI of Toulouse was convicted by the pope of living in murder, robbery, and flagrant disregard of all Christian principles. Ex- communication must follow.

What did immediately follow was the murder of the legate Peter, in January, 1208, at the court of Count Raymond, by an Albigensian; an Albigensian attached to the service of Raymond and befriended by him. This was the last straw; the climax to a long series of insults and injuries inflicted by the Albigensians on the Catholics of Languedoc. The time for action had come. Otherwise the heretics penetrating all Europe with insidious doctrines would destroy the faith of Christendom. To Pope Innocent went the appeal from French bishops and Cistercians. Only by the sword could Christian civilisation be saved from heretics that used the sword. Unless the Albigensians were exterminated they would exterminate the Catholics.

Innocent heard the appeal; recognising its urgency he proclaimed the crusade.

Threatened from without by Saracens in Palestine, by Moslems in Spain, Christendom was not to be disintegrated by the heretics—"pestilent fellows, who [in Innocent's words] seek not only our property but also our lives." War was the only alternative to the peace, fervently desired by Dominic and the pope.

War, a holy war, since by no other means could the Albigensian power be reduced. A crusade of forty days was approved by Philip Augustus—for his nobles; the king of France was too busy over his war with John of England and the Emperor Otto to turn south. Forty days was the customary limit of feudal service and french nobility and knighthood went briskly enough to a war blessed by the pope against the "pestilent" heretics. To go on this crusade brought the same privileges and pardons granted to crusaders against Moors and Saracens. It also promised reward in material things, rich spoils of war. To avoid unpleasantness, to put himself right in the eyes of Pope Innocent, Count Raymond promptly joined the crusade. It was a temporary expedient and it served Raymond's personal end.

Crusade Against the Albigenses

Two armies moved on Languedoc, one of them commanded by Simon of Montfort, the English earl of Leicester, holder of lands in northern France. The Albigenses had for allies a number of lesser nobles, robber lords who from their strongly built castles waged war on all who came their way. The crusaders carried all before them, taking Beziers by storm and a month later capturing the rocky fortress of Carcassonne. The fall of Beziers, attended by a general massacre of all its inhabitants, frightened waverers throughout the countryside; many whose sympathies were Albigensian declared for the crusade. The total number slain in Beziers cannot be set down with any sure accuracy, medieval figures in the absence of statistics are guess-work. Neither can the words alleged to have been spoken by Abbot Arnold at the time of the massacre be accepted as necessarily true. It is told by a contemporary writer[1] that the misgivings of some of the crusaders, fearful of killing Catholics in the promiscuous slaughter, were quieted by the Cistercian abbot's exhortation to "kill all; God will know His own." The words may have been uttered, we know not by whom, and then attributed to Abbot Arnold. It is more probable that an excited soldier, without any high sense of responsibility, shouted out the encouragement to "kill all." As an object lesson in military ruthlessness the massacre had immediate effect. It brought fear and submission; but no abiding love for the Catholic faith of the crusaders.

With the fall of Carcassonne the crusade, as far as most of the French knights and nobles were concerned, was over. They had routed the Albigenses and destroyed many of their strongholds. The heretics, no longer predominant in Languedoc, were a minority in the land. Knights and nobles protested they had done their feudal service and must needs return to look after their own estates in the north. Guerilla warfare in the wild mountainous country was the last thing that appealed to the chivalry of France. Such warfare might go on for years and years—as indeed it did. They must needs return, these feudal knights and nobles to civilisation, to attend to their private affairs; above all many longed for Paris. So they departed, leaving Simon of Montfort in command of the remnant of the army.

Earl Simon was not the man to turn back. To his English earldom of Leicester and French lordship of Montfort he added the viscounty of Beziers and Carcassonne and gave the full list of his titles when he wrote to Pope Innocent of the position in southern France; mentioning in the same letter that his soldiers would stay with him only because their pay had been doubled.

Henceforth the crusade became a struggle between Simon and Raymond VI for the mastery of the whole country and the overlordship of Toulouse. At every and any cost Raymond meant to remain count of Toulouse. He saw with misgivings the progress of Montfort's all-conquering army. After the fall of Carcassonne and the departure of the French nobility Raymond decided that his right place was at home. The crusade knew him no more. Back in Toulouse he resumed his old way of life, keeping on good terms with the Albigenses, raising money in his customary arbitrary fashion. When papal legates censured him and ecclesiastical councils threatened excommunication Raymond first appealed to the pope and then went to Rome to explain to Innocent how grossly he had been misrepresented, how profoundly misunderstood. In fact Raymond was a very ill-used man whose one desire was to serve the Church—according to the story he told Pope Innocent. And Innocent, always willing to believe the best of men, always meeting the sinner half-way when repentance was expressed, required him to go back to Toulouse and put things right with the legates.

Since putting things right involved a change of policy in

the government of Toulouse, which was the last thing Raymond contemplated, his excommunication long delayed was at length proclaimed. Pope Innocent, learning that Count Raymond had done nothing to amend his ways, that the charges of broken promises, of continued patronage of heretics, of violent disorderly conduct were unquestionably true, confirmed the sentence. This was in 1211. The war between Simon and Raymond now became a fierce and pitiless contest with deeds of ferocious savagery on both sides. Feudal law and custom complicated the relations of Catholics and Catharists in this war between Simon and Raymond. The latter, hard pressed, looking for allies, called on Peter, of the loose morals, king of Aragon, an overlord of lands on the French side of the Pyrenees, to come to his aid. Peter crowned by the pope in Rome, holding his kingdom as a vassal of the pope, was by no means inclined to have the victorious Simon from the north of France for a near neighbour. Before openly taking Raymond's side envoys from Peter went to Rome hoping to persuade Innocent to make peace in Languedoc and save the count of Toulouse from further molestation by Simon. But nothing could now be done for Count Raymond. He had gone too far in general lawlessness even for Innocent to save him. Church councils in France sent their legates to Rome with letters recounting Raymond's crimes against Catholics. It was the old story. Raymond would not give up his Albigensian heretics, would not refrain from attacks on Catholic prelates, nor would he yield to Simon of Montfort.

Then King Peter, intrepid soldier that he was, fresh from war against the Moors in Spain, with no mean part to his credit in that tremendous defeat of the Mohammedan armies on the high ground of Tolosa, decided that he must throw in his lot with Raymond rather than endanger the security of his Montpellier and Carcassonne land. Headstrong in all his ways; courageous in war, but too fond of making war; restive when

Innocent would restrain him, accounting himself a loyal son of the pope and devoted champion of the Church, yet with his incontinency and pride always a most troublesome son to his papal lord—King Peter of Aragon fell, tumbled to the dust, slain in that strange, unexpected and quite overwhelming victory of Simon's at the battle of Muret. It was but a year after Peter had shared at Las Navas in the honours of the Spanish triumph over the Moors when he was killed at Muret. Simon's army was ridiculously small compared with the forces of Count Raymond, and the rout and slaughter of the Albigensian army are hard to explain. Certain it is that Simon's cavalry swept all before them and suffered few casualties. Though Raymond escaped in the carnage, his cause was lost. For many years to come the Albigensians held out in their mountain fortress of Mont Segur but their power was broken; their influence steadily diminishing before the zeal of Dominican action. Unprotected in high places, for Raymond was deprived of his dominion and Pope Innocent granted the county of Toulouse to Earl Simon, to be held under the overlordship of the king of France, Albigensianism with its Manichean doctrine and aggressively anti-Catholic, anti-Christian ethics, ceased to threaten the civilisation of Europe. It languished in obscurity, all that was true fundamentally in the heresy to be reborn in the Church.

Waldensian Heresy

Far different from the Catharist heresy were the varying beliefs of the sects that concentrated on poverty and gradually, imperceptibly drifted away from the fellowship of the Catholic Church. The contrast between the magnificence, luxury, ostentatious pride and riches of ecclesiastical dignitaries and the poverty and humility of the Saviour of the world and His disciples arrested the minds of earnest men and women in the twelfth century. Reading and pondering the passages in the

New Testament that enjoined poverty and self-denial on the followers of Christ, they came in time, these earnest-minded people, to make poverty the one test of Christian life and to separate themselves from all who did not see eye to eye with them on the matter.

Peter Waldo, an originator of the movement in France, was venerated as the founder of the sect known as Waldenses. Waldo, himself a rich merchant of Lyons, was never a Waldensian. Contemporary writers describe Peter Waldo as a man of little learning but of great goodness of heart; a man who felt he must give his riches to the poor because God had called him to the following of Christ. Others joined him and soon an organisation—the Poor Men of Lyons—was created. A similar movement arose in Lombardy where the Poor Men were named Humiliati. In both cases the impulse to go out in the streets and highways and preach the gospel of poverty to all who would heed it was not to be disregarded. Untrained in theology the Poor Men went out as simple gospel preachers, and Pope Alexander III, the reigning pontiff, saw nothing objectionable in this evangelical work. On one condition Pope Alexander gave his sanction to the itinerant preachers. They must, he insisted, get the approval of the parish priest before they started preaching. It would never do to invade a parish without the consent of the priest in charge of the parish. Canon law, and Alexander III was the great exponent of canon law, did not allow the rights of the parish priest to be overlooked. Church order required obedience to the parish priest in all that pertained to his jurisdiction.

On this rule of Alexander III the Poor Men clashed with ecclesiastical authority and so, falling into heresy, departed from the Catholic communion. Here and there parochial clergy welcomed the gospel preachers of poverty but it was not to be expected that parish priests generally would approve the coming of strangers—laymen at that—whose message was a standing rebuke to the clerical habit of life. Far from exalting poverty, many a clerk in holy orders was greatly concerned with increasing his modest stipend, was in fact forever on the look-out for an opportunity to get a little richer. By such this gospel of poverty could hardly be received with sympathy. Parish priests, like the generality of mankind, found the message of the Poor Men entirely uncongenial and would have none of it in their hearing.

But the preachers were not to be restrained. Filled with confidence that the world needed their message, strong in the self-assurance that in their interpretation of the New Testament was the whole truth, these Poor Men of Lyons went their way; ignoring all authority of church and state, preaching where they would, affirming positively that no man should say them nay. Condemnation of these proceedings that struck at the root of all church order and discipline followed as a matter of course; first at the Council of Verona, 1184, and then at the Vatican Council of 1215. Pope Innocent found the Waldensians already far departed from orthodox belief. With separation from Catholic communion came repudiation of Catholic doctrine. The Waldensians decided that an ordained priesthood was unnecessary, the sacraments of the Church of no account. In their self-sufficiency they anticipated the sects of a later protestantism. In refusal to bear arms or take oaths, and no less in the simplicity of daily life and blameless personal character they foreshadow the Society of Friends.

For a while Poor Men and Humiliati—the two bodies never in agreement — spread their teaching to the disruption of the Catholic body, in France, Germany, and Italy; but the movement ultimately petered out, under pressure of the Inquisition, with burning for heresy of irreconcilables. Only in Piedmont did Waldensian congregations survive, enduring to our own day; prosperous, well-conducted communities, not greatly differing from other Protestant groups.

Franciscan Antidote

Heresy that would isolate an article of faith, an aspect of truth and make it the whole, denying all doctrine of a Catholic Church, divinely guided, inspired from the beginning; rejecting the Christian unity—one Lord, one Faith, one Baptism—cropped up throughout the twelfth century. The sanity of St. Francis of Assisi brought the doctrine of Christian poverty the sanction it needed. For St. Francis charity was the fundamental, the essential thing. Love brought him to espouse our Lady Poverty. What did poverty or self-mortification avail without charity? And this charity was all too obviously lacking in the sects that separated themselves in the name of poverty from the Catholic body. The spirit of separatism, the pride that condemned all who would not profess poverty, was something quite alien to the joyous flaming charity that filled the heart of St. Francis. Unlearned, no master of theology, not destined for the priesthood, poet and singer, Francis sought a common rule for his first companions, enlisted in a common cause. With the sanction of the pope, and without such sanction it never occurred to Francis to act, he and his brethren, bound together by a simple rule of life, would go out and preach to all mankind the glorious Gospel of Jesus Christ. (Like his contemporary St. Dominic and the later St. Ignatius Loyola, to preach to the unconverted Mohammedan was the first thought of St. Francis.)

Pope Innocent was disconcerted at their first meeting when Francis sought him out in the Vatican. Unaware of the character of the little poor man of Assisi, seeing in his visitor from Umbria yet another of the fanatical advocates of poverty, born it would seem to trouble the peace of the Church, Innocent abruptly dismissed him.

But when from Bishop Guido of Assisi, who had befriended Francis from the beginning, and from that very holy prelate Cardinal John of St. Paul, Innocent learnt what manner of man this new preacher was he at once discerned, at the second interview, that Francis was raised up to do the work of God. Innocent gave his verbal blessing to the Franciscan enterprise, and though formal recognition of a new religious order could not yet take place, any more than it could be done for Dominic and his preaching friars, the little band of friars minor had the papal approval. For Innocent knew the needs of Christendom; none knew these needs as he did. As in Dominic, so in Francis, Pope Innocent saw a man chosen and set apart for the renewal of Christian life in Europe. All that the heretics possessed of truth and goodness Dominic and Francis possessed. But besides that they had a burning love for the souls of men and the great charity that belongs to the supremely sane. They had wisdom, Dominic and Francis, wisdom that established the place of learning and poverty in the Catholic Church, wisdom that with charity would rout the pride of the heretics, and scatter the separatist arguments of sectaries.

So Innocent welcomed the coming of the friars, seeing in their founders messengers of peace. It was left to his successor to give formal approbation to the new order of friars minor.

Abbot Joachim of Flora

A figure remote from Dominic and Francis, still more remote from Peter Waldo, is the Cistercian monk Joachim, who after much travel in Europe and residence in Sicily as abbot of Corazzo, settled at Flora, first abbot of a new house of hermit monks. Learned, given to study, a man of prophetic contemplative mind, Joachim, with the approval of the popes immediately preceding Innocent, devoted himself to writing a commentary on the Bible. Not a work for popular consumption were the biblical studies of Joachim. No call reached this man of solitude and meditation to preach in public places or seek the conversion of the multitude. His personal sanctity earned respect for his writings, only to be withdrawn by authority when he had been many years dead; when the influence of those writings was becoming perceptible. Far more perceptible as the thirteenth century passed was the influence of Joachim's "Everlasting Gospel" on minds receptive of esoteric doctrine.

Joachim's meditations on the sacred scriptures brought him to the conclusion that in the Old Testament was revealed the rule of God the Father; an age of law and obedience through fear. The New Testament revealed the reign of God the Son; an age of grace and the loving obedience of sons. The third and new age was at hand, the reign of the Holy Ghost when liberty and charity would supersede the old commandments for: "the former things have passed away." In this period that was to come, and it was near at hand, Joachim was assured, the Jews would accept the Saviour, the Greeks would return to the unity of the Church, and the visible Church itself would be transformed into a Church invisible; the "Everlasting Gospel" would then be accepted as the interpretation of the Gospel of the New Testament. Announcement of the approaching end of the world, of cataclysmic or catastrophic change, always attracts certain minds. Without any special organisation to spread the "Everlasting Gospel" its prophetic message had an appealing force. Men believing the reign of the Holy Ghost to have begun, or to be at least at hand, grew impatient of the rule of priests and kings. An anti-clericalism was fostered.

Joachim was dead when Innocent had been but recently elected pope. There is nothing to suggest that Innocent was interested in the writings of the holy abbot of Flora. The papacy had troubles enough. Innocent, dealing with active heresy in Languedoc and nearer home, would not be concerned or excited over the mystical interpretations of a pious Cistercian writing in the quiet of his cell. Theologians at the Council of the Lateran, in 1215, found the explanatory theory of Joachim concerning the mystery of the Holy Trinity altogether defective and erroneous; the theory was condemned. But Joachim himself apart from his writings was not condemned. Later when movements hostile to the Catholic unity were seen in Europe, writings and sentiments were attributed to the author of the "Everlasting Gospel" that Joachim would certainly have not acknowledged.

Joachim of Flora belongs to the times of Innocent, though statesman and prophet were not to meet. Compared with heresies of Manichean, Catharists, and Waldensian separatists Joachim's "Everlasting Gospel" is the vision of a contemplative, whose imagination, dwelling on the things that are not seen, would have them visible. To Dante, Joachim was in the circle of the saints in Paradise, with Dominic and Anselm, and other blessed ones.[20]

---

[20] *Il Paradiso*, XII, 151.

CHAPTER IX
Relations with England

Vacancy at Canterbury—Stephen Langton—Interdict and Excommunication—Feudatory of the Pope—Magna Carta.

FROM his early years in Paris till his death Innocent was interested in England and kindly affectioned to its people. While a student at Paris he had journeyed to Canterbury to kneel as a pilgrim at the shrine of St. Thomas, the martyred archbishop, and thus is named with the few, the very few Roman pontiffs who have travelled in England. In one of Pope Innocent's earliest letters, sent to King Richard of the Lion-heart, the hope is expressed of visiting England again.

Richard of the Lion-heart had kingly qualities, recognisable by friend and foe. His successor, King John, was a ruler of different pattern altogether. Astute and without scruples was John. When it suited his policy he could play the Christian king, but no contemporary evidence suggests that he believed in the Christian religion or allowed a Christian conscience to influence private life or political action. In the eyes of this medieval monarch the Church in England was an instrument to be used for the king's purpose; its ministers dependent on the royal will, its revenues a constant source of wealth for the royal exchequer. It was said by those who were a lifetime in his service that only once did John receive the Holy Sacrament of the Lord's Body and Blood and that in boyhood. Such was the king of England with whom Pope Innocent was to deal. Much trouble he gave, did John to the pope, and to all who came in contact with him. For his word was not to be trusted and his heart was without compassion.

England was a prosperous country, when John came to the throne. This prosperity he devoured. In the first few years of his reign relations with the Holy See were disturbed, but not broken, by John's matrimonial infidelities and violations of ecclesiastical rights. Old Hubert Walter, Richard's justiciar, was archbishop of Canterbury and his long experience, political ability, and force of character gave him an influence that John could not disregard.[21] On Hubert's death in the summer of 1205 John, with frank satisfaction, exclaimed "Now, for the first time I am king of England." A synonym for "tyrant" was the word "king," since the throne of England was in John's view the seat of an absolute ruler, neither to be guided by counsel nor restrained by councillors. The authority of the pope was nothing to him. But at once, on archbishop Hubert's death, John found that the authority of Pope Innocent III was not lightly to be disregarded, was in fact a grave stumbling-block to enjoyment of absolute rule.

The succession at Canterbury brought the crisis. By canon law and right of ancient custom the monks of the chapter of Canterbury were privileged to name the man they would have for archbishop. Therefore immediately on Hubert's death not the whole cathedral chapter but the more active members got together, elected Reginald, their subprior, and sent him off to Rome to be consecrated by the pope and return with the pallium.

---

[21] Pope Innocent required the archbishop in to resign the justiciarship, but John made him chancellor. Archbishop Hubert belongs to the company of eminent civil servants drawn from the archiepiscopal throne of Canterbury.

On the other hand John knew that the king of England commonly told the Canterbury chapter whom they should elect for their archbishop and that the royal candidate nominated by the crown was the choice approved by the pope. John therefore promptly named for archbishop for Canterbury, with its great responsibilities, spiritual and political, a creature of his own, one John de Grey, bishop of Norwich, an ecclesiastic who could be trusted to do the king's will—to the detriment of the good estate of the Church. John could quote plenty of precedents for his action. William of Normandy had chosen Lanfranc for his archbishop; his son Rufus had named Anselm; Thomas Becket was the nominee of Henry II.[22] The archbishop of Canterbury stood so near to the crown, was in fact a great temporal lord, foremost in the royal councils, that John took it for granted the pope would accept his nominee. But John did not know Pope Innocent III. For Innocent, chief shepherd of Christendom, calmly set aside the choice of the coterie of monks and the choice of John. He had fixed on a far greater, far holier and more learned priest than subprior Reginald or the grossly complacent Bishop John de Grey. An Englishman, Stephen Langton, but recently made cardinal, was chosen by Innocent to be archbishop of Canterbury to the rage and indignation of King John. While the monastic chapter readily consented to the pope's choice, John swore he would have none of it. The papal letter announcing the appointment of Stephen Langton and describing him as one "than whom there was no man greater in the Roman court, nor was there, any equal to him in character and in learning" provoked John's fury beyond restraint. Learning and virtuous qualities were the last things the king looked for in so great a personage as an archbishop of Canterbury. On the pope's consecration of Langton at Viterbo in June, 1207, John fiercely retaliated, seizing the archbishop's

---

[22] When Henry VIII nominated Thomas Cranmer to the see of Canterbury, the Pope duly accepted the nomination and gave Cranmer the pallium.

estates at Canterbury, driving the monastic chapter into exile, and proclaiming that anyone who acknowledged Stephen as archbishop should be accounted a public enemy.

Thus did the king of England reply when the wise judgement of Innocent gave England one of its noblest and greatest archbishops.

Stephen Langton[23]

He came of a Lincolnshire family, Stephen Langton, and was but a few years younger than Innocent. A man after Innocent's own heart. The two had much in common. In their love of justice, of the order that comes of good law, in knowledge of and affection for the Bible, in the vocation for the active rather than the contemplative life—both men were akin. When estrangement came Innocent was puzzled, Langton understood and was patient.

Pursuing wisdom, seeking learning, Stephen went as a matter of course as a young man to Paris. There he stayed when the student years were passed, taking what we should call to-day his master's degree, and lecturing on moral theology and on the Sacred Scriptures. At Paris Master Stephen made his name, and his reputation grew and extended. He became famous as a preacher, at a time when preachers were rare, no less than as a professor in the schools. Devoting himself to the Latin text of the Bible, the Vulgate, he made that division into chapters which proved so much to the advantage of all Bible readers in the centuries to come. Revision and correction would amend Langton's arrangement in many places to-day but the practical value of that arrangement has stood a prolonged test of time. No dry-as-dust biblical commentator was Langton. The sacred books of Old and New Testaments were as daily food to him. Deep piety and poetic feeling are revealed in the hymn he

---

[23] Consult *Stephen Langton*, by F.M. Powicke, Oxford, 1928.

wrote, *Veni, Sancte Spiritus,* still sung as a sequence in the Mass for Whit Sunday and known to uncounted millions in its English translation, "Come, Thou Holy Spirit, Come." Authorship of that hymn has been attributed to Pope Innocent III and to King Robert. The evidence in favour of Stephen Langton is stronger; is sufficient indeed to establish his authorship. (At the same time the evidence is not overwhelming. Research does no more than convince most scholars that Stephen Langton and no other wrote *Veni, Sancte Spiritus.*)

Much has been preserved of the speech of Langton during his time in Paris; the character as it impressed contemporaries is not obscure. Greatly as he appreciated the religious life Langton was convinced that only in rare cases did monks make good bishops. (St. Hugh the Carthusian, bishop of Lincoln, was in that rare case; it fell to Stephen Langton as archbishop of Canterbury to report favourably on the cause for St. Hugh's canonisation. Among his predecessors, in the see of Canterbury, are Lanfranc and St. Anselm, Benedictine monks.) To the custom of parents solemnly dedicating their children to the religious life, a custom condemned by Pope Alexander III who ruled that a child so dedicated must be free to decide for himself at the age of fourteen, Langton was firmly opposed. The personal conviction that for him the active not the contemplative was the appointed life was shaken for a while when he lived in exile at the Cistercian abbey at Pontigny, and again when suspended by the papal legate he set out to Rome for the Lateran Council. Despondent at the apparent frustration of his plans and labours for the welfare of England, Archbishop Langton felt inclined to become a hermit or Carthusian, and it was left to Gerald of Wales to reprove his friend for thus yielding to depression. Nearly seventy was Gerald, and still as ready for argument and controversy—not to say intrigue and wire-pulling—as ever, when he wrote to Langton reminding the archbishop of convictions expressed in the Paris years. The life of a prelate was greater in dignity and influence than a hermit's, Gerald insisted. The former rules, the latter is ruled. St. Basil and St. Gregory were greater than Macarius or Anthony, for the talents we possess are to be put to useful service, not buried in the ground. The active life might not be as safe as the contemplative but yet it was in every way preferable. A queer, egotistical old man was Gerald the Welshman; loyal to his friends and affectionate; not wanting in courage, for he refused to serve King John at the time of the interdict. His writings are full of information concerning his times.

The mood that brought inclination to retire from the world passed. Stephen Langton was born not to be a spectator of passing events but for an active part in the public affairs of his time.

Problems of moral law interested the student and professor at Paris. As a pupil of a famous rigorist in ethics, Peter the Chanter, Langton discussed the question of usury, that is, the sin of covetousness, and the duty of restitution. Paris theologians felt strongly on the subject of interest on money loans. It was no mere academic discussion. Christian ethics were concerned with the conduct of traders charging more than a just price for the goods they sold; with lawyers demanding fees above the amount due to them; with ecclesiastics who built churches with money gained by usury. Abbeys and great churches like Notre Dame in Paris, erected in the latter half of the twelfth century, were paid for with money borrowed from money-lenders, Jewish and Christian. Certain moral theologians gave their opinion that an abbot enriched by the profits of money-lending should hand over to the bishop of the diocese benefactions from such tainted source that the ill-gotten gains might be restored to the usurer's victims. Restitution might leave the abbey without endowment but that was better than endowment through usury.

Caesar of Heisterbach mentions the case of a very wealthy money-lender in Paris, named Theobald, who became uneasy at being so rich and consulted the bishop as to what could be done about it. The bishop strongly advised Theobald to quiet his conscience by giving the money to the cathedral building fund. But Peter the Chanter, Langton's master, would have none of this trafficking with the unclean thing, and declared that every penny should go back to the people who had borrowed on usury from Theobald.

Usury was attacked because it was held to be a violation of natural law; and natural law being the moral law given by God to all mankind was therefore binding on all. Hence it was laid down that "no one is in a state of salvation who knowingly lives on the profit of usury." Robert Curzon, Langton's contemporary at Paris and later a fellow cardinal, urged that a general council of bishops and princes should be held with the pope presiding, to decree, once and for all, that "everyone must work, either with soul or body, in order that everyone may eat the bread of his own labour as the Apostle commanded; so that no parasitic or idle (*curiosi*) folk dwell among us, and all usurers, mischief-makers and idlers would be done away."

Stephen Langton was not a profound theologian; neither was he an original thinker. But he was aware of the development of theology and of morals. Amid the intellectual ferment in Paris, the vital discussions—followers of Abelard contending with followers of St. Bernard on principles of law and the nature of the Real Presence in the Holy Eucharist, no less than on ethics, with a steady use of dialectic growing up—in this environment Langton learnt the first principles of political justice and acquired the habit of clear statement. His chief work in Paris was always to lecture on the Sacred Scriptures and his commentaries, while not concerned with textual criticism, abound in allegorical interpretation. Innocent knew him well, this Englishman; having brought him to Rome and made him cardinal he saw him as the very man to fill the vacant see of Canterbury. The essential thing for Pope Innocent was in every case to have the right man elected. The general law of the Church, the canon law, that gave to chapters the election of bishops, was not to be a stumbling-block. Innocent approved the law as he accepted nominations of princes. But he was chief shepherd of Christendom and Christian statesman. The archbishopric of Canterbury must not be awarded as a prize to the favourite of chapter or prince. There was no one comparable to Cardinal Stephen Langton, no one more fitted to be England's foremost prelate. The pope was confident that his appointment of Stephen Langton was the best possible thing for the English people. His confidence was justified, though the appointment brought a sea of troubles on clergy and laity of England when the fury of England's king was unloosed.

Interdict and Excommunication

Innocent laid all England under an interdict when John, ignoring completely papal warnings and remonstrances, continued to plunder the archbishop's estates and threaten the archbishop with death should he land. It fell heavily on the common people, this interdict, since it meant an end to the public ministrations of religion and remained in force for more than five years. To John it brought opportunity for fresh onslaughts on the Church. No sooner was the interdict published, the bells silenced, than John declared all ecclesiastical property, monastic or secular, confiscated to the crown. There was no one to say him nay. The barons were willing enough to see the king's treasury filled at the expense of the clergy; of the bishops only two were left in England; Peter des Roches of Winchester, a warlike prelate, always the agent of foreign interests, and John de Grey of Norwich—supple tools of the king. The turn of the laity came next when John, not content with church property, confiscated where he would. To Matthew Paris, the St. Albans chronicler, "it seemed as though the king was courting the hatred of every class of his subjects, so burdensome was he to rich and poor."

One more chance of amendment was given to John before Innocent pronounced sentence of excommunication on this contumacious king. Pandulf the papal legate was sent to England with peace proposals. Let the king restore the property of the clergy, let him receive Stephen Langton, cardinal archbishop, with his kinsmen and friends and the rest of the exiled bishops "fairly and in peace," and the interdict should be lifted. The interdict did not trouble John, receive the archbishop he would not. So that for the time was the end of Pope Innocent's peace proposals. Pandulf had no choice but to pronounce the sentence of excommunication; which he did in the presence of the whole council of the realm. By this sentence all John's subjects were released from their allegiance to the king and commanded to give obedience to whomsoever should be sent as John's successor.

For a while John treated the excommunication with cheerful contempt; with an army of continental mercenaries, ravaging and plundering he took his lawless way. But his position was fast becoming precarious, for the barons, and especially the northern barons, tired of being robbed were plotting John's overthrow and it was known that Philip of France had papal sanction to depose the king of England and reign in his stead. John stopped the French invasion, to Philip's exceeding annoyance, by a change of policy. He surrendered to the pope at the end of 1212 and in the spring of the following year Pandulf the legate was once more in England. Before the legate and "the great men of the realm" John solemnly swore to fulfil all the pope's demands, to receive Stephen as archbishop and recompense the clergy for their losses.

Feudatory of the Pope

But John was not giving up the policy of absolute rule without getting something worth having in exchange. Interdict and excommunication were of no account in his eyes. To show of personal humiliation, to the humiliation of crown and country, he was entirely indifferent. By a formal surrender of the whole realm of England and Ireland,[24] "to God and to the holy Mother Church of Rome, and to Pope Innocent and his Catholic successors," in the knowledge that he would hold the realm thenceforth as "a feudatory of God and the Roman Church," John decided that he bound the pope by a tie that would ensure papal protection. Now he could count on the pope to stand by him against rebellious barons. It was a small price to pay, this act of humiliation that meant nothing, for the gain of papal friendship and assurance that the danger of French invasion was ended. As one of the English chroniclers, Walter of Conventry, wrote—"for when once he had put himself under apostolical protection and made his realms a part of the patrimony of St. Peter, there was not in the Roman world a sovereign who durst attack him or would invade his lands, in such awe was Pope Innocent held above all his predecessors for many years past."

No evidence suggests that Innocent asked for or even desired the homage of the king of England. The barons supported the surrender because they believed the papal overlordship would impose restraint on John and at the same time save the country from war.

(Matthew Paris has a story—but what Matthew Paris wrote is not always to be believed—that John was willing to pay homage and tribute to the Mohammedan emir of Morocco, so

---

[24] Pope Innocent never regarded Ireland as part of the realm of England. He sent legates there as he did to Scotland and the reports of his legates throw light on the abuses in the Irish Church.

anxious was he for an alliance with some foreign power.)

Stephen Langton had no illusions. Knowing the character of the king he had warned the barons years before that John was breaking both the law and doctrine of the Church, violating his coronation oath. The archbishop, in exile at Pontigny, had urged the barons to stand for justice, reminding them that his predecessor St. Thomas had died rather than yield to royal absolutism. (Pontigny was full of the memory of St. Thomas, for there he, too, had lived in exile.) Stephen Langton had no illusions about King John. No change of heart was to be expected, no matter the submissions to the pope and professions of obedience.

Innocent on the other hand was content to accept John's submission and the overlordship of England as a surrender made in good faith, an act of obedience on the part of a penitent man. Feudalism brought these relations of ruler and vassal. They were customary relations in a society that recognised other and higher relations, a society subject to a higher law. Pope Innocent accepted the feudal system of his time not as a divine institution but as a human device that did with more or less success bind rulers and subjects together. At the prayer of Queen Constance the pope, for the safeguarding of the queen's small child Frederick, had received the overlordship of the kingdom of the Sicilies and the responsibility had not been shirked. Over more than one ruler in Spain and Portugal was the pope the feudal overlord. There was nothing that appeared to Innocent unusual, nothing to astonish him in the king of England promising amendment of life and, freed from excommunication, making the pope his feudal lord.

But Pope Innocent could not know the character of John — as Langton knew it. Neither John's cleverness, nor his vigorous contempt for all who crossed his path, neither his utter want of feeling where the welfare of others was concerned, nor his ready capacity to break his word did Pope Innocent realise. The character of John, king of England, was something that Innocent for all his experience of European princes could not estimate at its true value. The frank and open revolt against papal authority on the part of princes was no new thing in European politics. Its persistence brought excommunication; so grave a sentence as excommunication commonly reduced the offender to penitence. Hence Pope Innocent saw the abject surrender of John as the mark of penitence; knowing Europe as he did and England so little, he could hardly see it otherwise. That archbishop Stephen, Innocent's friend did not regard John in the same light, but should still see him an impenitent tyrannical ruler, the pope simply could not understand. Inevitably estrangement came between pope and archbishop.

The papal legate made matters more difficult for the archbishop. For the legate, being an Italian, quite ignorant of English customs and as ready as the pope to take John's word for the word of a truly penitent king, filled up vacant bishoprics and benefices on his own initiative without consulting the archbishop. However, when the legate was recalled to Rome and John, after publicly proclaiming that there should be no further interference in church appointments, departed to France on his last and disastrous campaign to recover the Angevine provinces, Stephen Langton set to work to bring the barons together and persuade them to enforce public order.

The national grievances in England were really enormous and intolerable. The whole administration of justice was corrupt. No one could be sure how the arbitrary decisions of the king's officers would be carried out. Liberty of the subject was a farce when freemen could be arrested, evicted from their lands, exiled and outlawed without legal warrant or fair trial. The entire system of government and administration set up under the Norman kings, and developed in the reigns of Henry and Richard, had been turned by John's cunning into an instrument of oppressive extortion, that spared neither man nor woman. All classes of the nation from the earl to the villein suffered under John's pitiless tyranny. Here and there the barons had struck against some act of personal injury. The northern barons had shown conspicuous resentment, refusing to follow John, their liege lord, in his military expeditions to France. But there was no cohesion among them, nor any sense of national wrong to be righted, until Archbishop Stephen, fully conscious of the responsibility laid on the successor of Lanfranc and Anselm, of Theobald and Thomas the martyr, took the lead with a resolute will to end the royal despotism. To the archbishop it was something more than a struggle between a tyrannical king and a set of turbulent nobles. Stephen Langton's effort was to win recognition of law for *all* men and to restore some measure of justice and the enjoyment of fair liberty throughout the land. As the archbishop saw it, the barons by contending for their own rights were really contending for the rights of all freemen.

John met the demands of the barons "for the laws and liberties of the charter of King Henry I" (including a threat of war if the demand was refused), with evasive non-committal replies. Then finding himself deserted by barons and ecclesiastics John appealed to his liege lord the pope against his "rebellious subjects"; at the same time declaring himself a crusader and taking the cross. Innocent sent letters to the barons rebuking them for conspiracies and conjurations and also to John telling him to harken to "just petitions," but the barons stood firmly by their oath: war or the charter of laws and liberties.

Magna Carta

Finally on June 15, 1215, in the meadow called Runnymead, between Staines and Windsor, in the presence of Archbishop

Stephen and seven bishops, of nearly the whole baronage and "a multitude of most illustrious knights," the Great Charter, *Magna Carta* was sealed. It was in the main but the old charter of Henry I writ large. It set up no new rights, conferred no new privileges, sanctioned no constitutional changes, proclaimed no new liberties. The real importance of Magna Carta is the fact that it was a *written* document, the first great act which laid down in black and white the main points of the constitution and the several rights and duties of king and people. To Cardinal Archbishop Langton belongs the credit for the sealing of the Great Charter, the cardinal archbishop whom Pope Innocent had appointed. With the sealing of the charter and its publication within a week throughout England "a sort of peace (*quasi pax*) was made between the king and the barons"—as an English chronicler[25] put it.

    The peace thus patched up was not to last. The barons no more trusted the king than the king trusted the barons. John had already appealed to his lord the pope, representing himself as a zealous crusader hindered from going overseas by the conduct of disloyal subjects, receiving in reply a general condemnation of all disturbers of the peace. Certain barons were named as incurring excommunication for disobedience to the pope's vassal. The legate Pandulf once more in England allying himself with John's episcopal supporter, the warlike Peter des Roches of Winchester, now called on the archbishop to enforce these excommunications. But the archbishop demurred. He was about to set out for Rome to attend the general council which the pope had called. In Rome he would discuss the whole matter with the pope. Busy over the preparations for the general council, Pope Innocent entirely misunderstood the situation in England—so it appeared to Archbishop Stephen Langton. Thereupon Pandulf the

---

[25] Ralph of Coggeshall.

legate—an ill choice for England—backed by Peter des Roches, declaring by virtue of his authority Stephen Langton disobedient to the papal mandate pronounced him suspended from the office of archbishop. Langton made no protest against the sentence. He quietly departed to Rome and was present at the general council that assembled in November. For the time his work in England was over. The charter had been sealed at Runnymead. King and barons were at civil war, the country laid waste by John's foreign mercenaries, the barons praying Louis, the son of Philip of France, to come over and take the English crown.

Pope Innocent declared the Charter annulled on the ground that since both king and barons had made the pope overlord of England no change could be made in the government and constitution without the pope's consent. But this disallowing of the Charter was never formally published in England, for the legate, the primate and the rest of episcopate were all at Rome for the council.

The sentence of suspension was removed from Stephen Langton in February, 1216. A few months later and Innocent III was dead. In the following October John was dead.

Stephen Langton was back at Canterbury the following year to remain for eleven years more the primate of England, to fulfil in those years the work Innocent III had summoned him to fulfil. As for the papal overlordship that John had secured, England had no use for it. The English baronage never held the pope as its overlord after John's career was ended. It was left to Edward I to find the papal overlordship inadmissible and England no fief of the Holy See.

CHAPTER X
Fourth General Council of the Lateran

Constitution of the Council—Canons of the Council—Relics and Indulgences—The Jewish Question.

POPE INNOCENT crowned the work of his life when he summoned a general council of the Church. It was to assemble in Rome, in November, 1215, and in order that ample time might be given to all concerned as early as April, 1213, were the letters sent that called to the council bishops and abbots, heads of religious orders, temporal princes and representatives of free cities and republics.

This was the fourth general council to meet in Rome within a hundred years. In his youth Innocent had been keenly aware of the general council of 1179 called by Pope Alexander III; the third general council of the Lateran.

The historic ecumenical councils of earlier centuries, required as they were to define some article of the Catholic faith, to affirm true Christian doctrine in the face of misrepresentation or misunderstanding, met in the East—at Nicea, Constantinople, Chalcedon, Ephesus. As the political influence of the "New Rome" of Constantinople dwindled and the Holy Roman Empire of Charlemagne emerged in the West with the papacy recognisably the centre of Christendom it was in the natural order that the pope should bring together the bishops from all parts of the Christian world, call them to meet in Rome, the city of the Apostles. Not primarily to define dogma were they now called but rather to amend moral disorders within the Church, correct abuses and declare positive principles for the better conduct of the Catholic people of God—clergy and laity.

So it was that Innocent called that fourth general council of the Lateran—by far the largest, most representative, and altogether most important of all the medieval general councils of the Church. In addition to the urgent need of reform within the Church Innocent would have common action taken against the encroaching power of Islam and the spread of the Albigensian heresy; he also desired to see the political struggle for the empire adjusted by the common and united voice of Catholic Christendom. Thus Innocent declared his mind when he sent out letters and commanded his numerous legates to bid all who were invited to be present in Rome on the first day of November, a.d. 1215.

Constitution of the Council

To Rome they came in the autumn of that last year of Innocent's life, so that it was said the whole world seemed to be there. (It was also reported that so great was the pressure in Rome that people were actually crushed to death.) Four hundred and twelve bishops, including the Latin patriarchs of Constantinople and Jerusalem, were present, with the episcopate of every country of Europe represented except the far-off Scandinavian lands. But few in number were the bishops from Germany because the war between Otto and Frederick II was still being waged when the summons to the council was issued. Eight hundred abbots and priors, with the heads of religious orders, Cistercian, Premonstratensian, Knights Templar and Hospitaller and proctors chosen by cathedral chapters, collegiate churches, and bishops unable to attend. Temporal rulers responded to the pope's invitation. Otto the excommunicated no less than Frederick II was represented. So were Philip Augustus of France and John of England. Kings of Hungary, Aragon, and Cyprus and the Latin emperor of Constantinople sent ambassadors. The republican states of Milan and Genoa, with other free cities of Italy, had their appointed delegates at this memorable ecumenical gathering, called by Pope Innocent III and assembled under Innocent's presidency.

Three formal public sessions of the council were held. They took place at the opening of the council on November 11, on November 20, and at the close of the council on November 30. At numerous committee meetings before the formal opening of the council and between the public sessions canons and decrees were drawn up that, when finally passed, would be sent out to the whole Catholic world. Disciplinary laws for the better government of the Church were many of these canons—in some cases to bind the faithful, clerk and laity, for all time.

Innocent preached at the opening of the council, deploring in his sermon the unhappy condition of Palestine, where the Saracens triumphed over Christians and held them in bondage. If the council wished him to do so the pope would himself set out to rouse the nations that the Holy Land might be free. "All of us who are priests," the pope insisted, "must be ready to lay down our lives and give up all earthly goods for the sacred cause." But the first and crying need was the reform of personal life. From the laxity of the clergy came the evils that beset Christian nations. "Faith perishes, religion is deformed, liberty brought to confusion, justice flouted, while heretics flourish, schismatics multiply and the Saracens, sons of Agar the bondwoman, triumph"—because of the sinful shortcomings of the Christian priesthood.

This to Pope Innocent was the root of the matter: personal amendment of life. Evil and unworthy conduct of men who should be examples was the plague of Christendom, the scandal of the world.

At the public sessions approval of a fresh crusade was expressed, claims of Frederick II to the imperial throne approved, English barons in arms against John, the pope's vassal, declared excommunicated as rebels, and the suspension of Stephen Langton, cardinal archbishop of Canterbury confirmed because he had supported the "rebels." (There is no record of any protest by the archbishop. Calmly he waited for Innocent to annul the suspension, and this was done early in February, 1216). These decisions on topical events are not conciliar decrees. They are judgements *ad hoc,* general endorsements of the pope's policy and aims. Only on one or two points did the council dissent from Innocent's opinion.

On the question of Earl Simon's possession of the lands of Raymond VI of Toulouse, the council favoured Simon's title holding him to be rightful lord of the county which he had won from the heretical and entirely untrustworthy Raymond, while Pope Innocent, still hoping for better things from Raymond, argued against the absolute grant of spoils to the victor. In the end the compromise was effected that gave Simon lordship of Toulouse, but conditionally, as vassal of the king of France.

Another matter that revealed sharp difference of opinion between the pope and the council was the provision of financial help for the papacy. What Innocent wanted was an in-: come for the Holy See that would make the pope independent of temporal rulers; at the same time delivering him from the necessity of charging high fees for the legal business transacted in the papal curia. The avarice of Rome is a common accusation throughout the Middle Ages, repeated as often as not without any evidence to justify the reproach. But the truth, and Innocent was fully aware of it, was that. without the fees obtained from suitors at the papal court, fees that mounted up in law costs and increased with every postponement and vexatious delay, the poverty of the Holy See was appalling.

When the pope had private resources he could afford to live on the narrow means of the papacy without inconvenience; but it remained an intolerable condition this dependence on personal property, favouring the election to the papacy of members of the wealthy families of Rome. With government of the Church centralised in the papacy—and this centralisation Innocent himself regarded as a necessary development of good order—the urgency of financial reform that would secure an adequate income for the pope seemed evident. Evident was this at least to Pope Innocent; less evident to the majority of the council when it came to a discussion of Innocent's plan for a steady income for the papacy.

Since from every land of Christendom came appeals to Rome, Innocent proposed that a tenth of its revenue should be assigned by every cathedral to the support of the Holy See. This scheme appeared reasonable to a considerable number of bishops and they spoke in support of it. But the opposition would have none of it. An annual contribution from each diocese known as Peter's Pence that did not fall exclusively on the clergy was one thing. Innocent's proposal quite another. For the latter meant a tax levied on episcopal incomes. It provoked strong dislike; usually expressed in every age when a direct tax on income is announced. The dislike was articulate at the general council of the Lateran, a.d. 1215, and Innocent rather than have it thought that his scheme was a vital reason for the summons of the council withdrew it. (But there would be much trouble, in England in especial, in the near future because of this refusal to arrange an income for the pope.)

The canons and decrees of the council, seventy in number,[26] were formally published and confirmed at the last open session. Many of these canons are of historical interest, revealing medieval troubles.

---

[26] A full list of these canons may be found in Hefele's *Councils*, edited by Leclerecq.

Others are restatements of earlier decrees of the Church. Taken in all, the canons and decrees of the council provide a summary of the problems that Innocent decided must be answered positively and definitely, enumerate existing evils in the Church, call attention to the tares to be uprooted, to the clerical habits and customs not tending to edification.

Canons of the Council

In its first canon the council plainly and clearly set down the fundamentals of Catholic doctrine travestied or denied by Albigenses and by the numerous sects that existed outside the Church. God and God alone created all things in heaven and earth, the devil created nothing; the existence of evil comes from misdirected will. Jesus Christ, the only-begotten Son of God, took human flesh and became Incarnate of the Virgin Mary. This the Christian Church has always believed and for the believers in the Christian faith there is but one Church, the Church founded by Jesus Christ. Outside the Church there is no salvation.

This same first canon also declares the Catholic doctrine concerning the sacraments of Baptism and the Holy Eucharist. Baptism may be validly administered by any one who uses water and the right formula; its grace is given to little children as certainly as to adults. Sins committed after baptism are forgiven on repentance and on doing penance. The sacrament of the altar, wherein our Lord Jesus Christ is both priest and victim, can only be celebrated by priests properly ordained. To none but the Apostles and their successors did Christ give the power to make priests. The mystery of Christ's real presence in the Eucharist is affirmed; the word transubstantiation is used for the first time in defining the consecration of the bread and wine that turns the elements into the body and blood of Christ—*transubstantiatis pane in corpus et vino in sanguinem*—so runs the canon.

The false puritanism of the Albigenses with its abhorrence of Christian marriage is condemned emphatically by this same canon; which maintains that in the chastity of monks and nuns and no less in true married life is the way to eternal happiness found. To say that marriage is a barrier to salvation is heresy.

The great bulk of the canons of the council disclose current scandals and irregularities in the ecclesiastical order and are enactments for reform and correction. There are priests living in open sin with mistresses and concubines: they must be suspended from the performance of clerical duties, and if they take no notice of the suspension must be deposed. As for bishops who allow these scandals to continue, even in some cases taking money from the offender and leaving him alone, they are to be deprived of all episcopal authority without hope of reinstatement.

Then there is heavy drinking in clerical circles and bishops are among those who sit up all night carousing. It is known that organised drinking bouts take place, clergy competing with clergy in the consumption of intoxicants and endeavouring to out-drink one another. What is the result of this drunkenness? The absence from choir of priests who should be at Matins, inability to say Mass. Some bishops indeed rarely say Mass at all and make light of the very idea of assisting at Mass. When these prelates do assist they behave without decorum, hardly attending to the service, choosing rather to talk with laymen and discuss diocesan business.

The sporting cleric, forever hunting and fowling, is also required to amend his way of life. Henceforth no matter how high his position in the hierarchy of the Church the keeping of hounds for the chase, of birds for hawking is forbidden the priest.

A list of occupations unseemly for a priest and therefore prohibited is given in another canon. The clergy must not be employed in trade, more particularly in trades of questionable honesty; they must not take part in stage performances; they must not gamble at dice, nor even be spectators at games of chance. They are not to have any part in legal trials at law where the penalty is the death sentence, nor be present as lookers-on at public executions. All military employment is strictly forbidden, and the practice of surgery prohibited. When travel makes it necessary, and on such occasions only, may the clergy make use of taverns. The tavern is absolutely out of bounds as a place for drinking and social intercourse. As to the customary priestly blessing of trials by ordeal, this must cease. Trials by ordeal were no Christian thing.[27]

The council also felt that some regulations ought to be enforced concerning the dress of the clergy. Clerks in minor orders, men who would never arrive at the priesthood but could plead their clergy rights when in trouble with authority—and some of them were forever getting into trouble—went attired in every kind of gay if ragged clothing as they wandered over Europe on their way to the schools of learning, and to the University of Paris above all. Parochial and cathedral clergy too often gravely offended in their extravagant and fantastic dress; making themselves conspicuous with bright colours. The time had not yet come when a uniform and sober clerical dress would be the rule, but the council made a start in that direction by positively forbidding all clerks in holy orders to go out in red and green. Moderation was also enjoined as to the length and cut of clerical coat. A happy mean between the

---

[27] Ordeal was a manifestation of the belief that God would not allow the conviction of an innocent person. It was of great antiquity, certainly pre-Christian. Wager by combat, in the dual, was the Norman form. Ordeal proper, in its many different ways, was Germanic and Anglo-Saxon. Its origin was due to the fact that no idea of evidence, such as we now understand this, existed at the time. It was formally condemned by the Church in the twelfth century and later.

coat or cloak that was obviously too long and a similar garment obviously too short must be found; and worn fastened at the neck. The ostentations of wealthy clerks, displayed on horseback in elaborate and expensive equipment, must be corrected. No longer could it be allowed that spurs, bridles, saddles, or any part of the harness should be gilded; and from henceforth let no gold or silver be used to decorate or ornament the bridles and belts of mounted clerks. Embroidered gloves and shoes, greatly fancied by clergy given to vanity, were by this canon of the council ordered to be worn no more. The priest as dandy and man of fashion must be suppressed.

To raise the standard of clerical life Pope Innocent and the council struck at the heart of the disease. The character of candidates for the priesthood called for attention. Far greater care was needed when appointments and preferments of the clergy were considered. Bishoprics were often left unfilled because cathedral chapters could not agree on the choice of a candidate, or were too negligent of their duty to elect. This bad state of things, the council decided, must cease. A whole series of canons is devoted to the reform of episcopal appointments. When a see is vacant for three months because the cathedral chapter has failed in its duty to elect—and a simple majority was sufficient to elect—then it is the duty of the metropolitan archbishop to fill the vacancy. It is also the duty of the metropolitan to confirm elections and conscientiously to examine the qualifications of the bishop elect. Grave penalties are incurred by a metropolitan who confirms the choice of an illiterate, a clerk of evil life or under the canonical age; the confirmation is itself invalid. To guard against undue influence of political power in the appointment of bishops the council decreed that elections made under such influence were of no account. The person so elected is further disqualified from all preferment in the future, while the electors forfeit their rights, besides incurring all loss of office and emoluments for the next three years.

The correction of abuses rather than their denunciation being the purpose of the decrees of the council, there is no avoidance of details in the canons. Abuses exist; they are a cause of scandal and grave injury to the whole body of the Christian Church, a stumbling-block to unbelievers. Therefore the abuses to be corrected are set out in the plainest language. No excuse of ignorance of the law can be pleaded when the law is clear to all. Fully aware of its responsibilities this great council did not ride off on moral platitudes or shrink from definite if disagreeable tasks by taking refuge in vague, high-sounding general statements; it tackled its appointed work in workmanlike manner, neglecting no item of ill-doing in its program of reforms, prescribing for the cure of evils, small and great, that were too conspicuously present in the Christendom Pope Innocent shepherded.

Clerical rapacity required a number of canons for its correction; in so many ways did that common human failing — to St. Paul a root of all evil—the love of money distract the faithful from the love of God and neighbour. The holding of more than one benefice by the same clerk, a practice forbidden by the previous Lateran Council of 1179, must not continue. In spite of its prohibition the "shameless greed" of men persisted in this nefarious pursuit of riches; the acquisitive spirit adding benefice to benefice. The council prescribed a remedy: acceptance of a second living required surrender of the first; the patron of the first living must without delay appoint a successor when a second living has been accepted.[28]

---

[28] But the "shameless greed" of men in holy orders was not exterminated by these admirable conciliar decrees. Three hundred years after Pope Innocent's council an English cardinal, one Thomas Wolsey, accumulated more high and rich ecclesiastical appointments in Great Britain than any priest had done before him or would do after him. (The established Church of England would also suffer the curse of pluralism.)

Fourth General Council of the Lateran

The bishops must see to it when they met in their annual provincial councils that appointments to benefices were properly made, reviewing all such appointments and in especial noting with disapproval episcopal preferment of unworthy clerks. Finally, on no account must the son of a canon, whether born in wedlock or illegitimate, be given a canonry in a church where his father is already canon.

Bishops also are told they must stop fleecing their clergy, retaining as they did too often the greater part of parochial incomes in their gift and leaving the unfortunate parish priest to exist on the wretched pittance left. They must also stop fleecing their clergy by demanding high fees at episcopal visitations, consecrations, and ordinations.

A livelier sense of duty was required in many bishops convicted of neglecting their obligation to preach, and no less convicted of neglecting the obligation to arrange for the education of the clergy in their diocese. In every cathedral and collegiate church—so had it been decreed by the Council of 1179—instruction should be given in theology and in the training of clergy for the priesthood. But in how many dioceses this decree had been entirely ignored, with the result that illiterate priests were found! Far better to have few good priests than many bad ones, the Council declared—an opinion that St. Thomas More would express in his day in similar words.

The religious orders, by demanding money from men called to be monks, women called to be nuns, came under censure at the Council. In future there must be no compulsory payment of dowry or premium.

Relics and Indulgences

Surveying as it did under Pope Innocent's direction the weak spots in the religious life of Christendom, the Council made rules for the suppression of the trade in sham relics.

Veneration of the relics of saints, like the reverence for holy places, is instinctive in mankind. (Perverted morbid taste will even desire the relics of great criminals.) With the growth and extension of the Christian Church the natural piety that would preserve some fragment of the weapon or clothing of a departed hero, that revered the burial place or tomb of prophet, priest, and king, that clung to the poor shreds endeared to the living by intimate association with the dead, was renewed and found fresh outlet.

Paganism and superstition comingle with natural piety and are hardly to be eliminated. Cupidity traded on human credulity in the Middle Ages, as it does today. The professional hawker of fraudulent relics became a common figure in medieval Christendom—portrayed for all time in Chaucer's Pardoner of the *Canterbury Tales*. Supply in every age meets the demand for the antique. Faked furniture, faked books, faked manuscripts, bought and sold as "genuine antiques"—we have known them all in the twentieth century. They were simpler, the sham relics of the travelling pedlar of the twelfth and thirteenth centuries. No elaborate pains were spent in disguising what appeared to the sceptic as plain pig's bones, but offered as bones of saints they found purchasers. The trade was too well organised, far too profitable to be extinguished. Since the demand for relics rested on a common human instinct, not in itself to be condemned but to be sublimated, the unholy commerce was the abuse. True reverence for the relics of saints kindled livelier Affection for the things of God. How to save this tender respect for true relics of the saints from exploitation by the mercenary and unscrupulous huckster was the problem for the council. Unable completely to make an end of the nefarious business a canon was passed—the sixty-second—forbidding any new relic to be exposed for veneration unless it had first been declared authentic by the Holy See.

Akin to the swindlers hawking faked relics and too often

imposing on pious souls were the itinerant collectors for charity, begging alms from the faithful for the crusade or other good cause and putting what they received in their own pockets. In future to guard against this particularly shabby form of robbery all collectors must be licensed, and carry with them letters authorising their appeal for funds. Further, these collectors being clerks in minor orders, were required to dress soberly and live uprightly, as became men engaged in religious work.

The granting of indulgences by bishops also needed strict attention. Far too many indulgences of an extravagant kind came from an episcopate lacking sense of responsibility in this grave matter.[29] But the right of a bishop to grant an indulgence was not denied.

Rules for the Laity

Ecclesiastical abuses were not confined within clerical

---

[29] A very distinguished present-day historian—not himself a Catholic—has admirably expressed how the doctrine of indulgences was liable to abuse in medieval Christendom—"In its purest form the theory underlying the indulgence was a fine one. It was inspired by the writings of St. Paul and was safeguarded by the maxim of the Fathers, *Quod homo non punit, Deus punit*. The system itself was a natural development of the penitential system and was related to the power of absolution. Its justification was found, in the climax of a long discussion among the canonists and theologians, in the doctrine of the treasure stored up by the saints and martyrs and all good Christians, who, a great body of friends, combine to help the erring. But it was extremely difficult to avoid misconception and abuse. Some of the theological terms, notably the term 'remission of sins,' was misleading; some of the preachers of indulgences were ignorant or headstrong or unscrupulous. Warfare had constantly to be waged by bishops and universities against the belief that not punishment, but sin itself, was remitted. ... The system encouraged fantastic and heterodox views about the unlimited powers of the pope, or profitless discussions on the nature of purgatory." Prof. F.M. Powicke, *The Christian Life in the Middle Ages*, Oxford, 1935.

circles. Lay patrons of church livings were known to appoint clerks to benefices and then keep most of the endowment for their own use, leaving the parish priests to exist on a miserable pittance. In fact some lay patrons simply farmed out to the lowest bidder benefices in their gift. This diversion of church property to lay purposes was altogether wrong—the Council pointed out—utterly against the law. Church patronage was a solemn responsibility, not an opportunity for personal gain on the part of the lay patron.

Tithe was not always paid with alacrity by laymen; sometimes notoriously it was never paid. By a whole series of evasions, postponements, and excuses the tithe payer escaped the tax. All that the Council could do was to declare the nature of the obligation of the landholder to make this payment. The tithe was the first charge laid on every landholder; it came before all other taxes were invented and it should be paid first.

The spiritual shortcomings of the laity were not overlooked by the Council. Year in and year out some lay folk neither went to the sacrament of Penance for absolution of their sins, nor knelt at the Table of the Lord to receive the Bread of Life. Frequent reception of Holy Communion was not the custom in Catholic Christendom in those medieval centuries. Weekly communion was the exception rather than the rule for clergy and laity. Pope Innocent sought a minimum for Christian men and women, and the Council fixed that minimum at once a year. Henceforth let every Catholic make confession annually at least to his parish priest—unless he has permission to make it elsewhere—and let him annually at least receive the Blessed Sacrament of the Body of Christ. And let Easter be the statutory time for the fulfilment of this duty. The Christian who did not comply with this rule of confession and communion at Easter, not being hindered by valid cause, fell by this very noncompliance under excommunication while living, and dying excommunicate must be refused Christian burial.

With this rule of confession for the laity went a stern injunction on the priest who heard confessions, strictly to keep silence concerning all that was told him in the confessional. The "seal of confession" must on no account be broken by the confessor. Violation of the silence imposed brought heavy penalties on the priest who so offended. Deprived of his benefice he must suffer a life sentence in a monastery of severe observance. From certain grave sins no absolution could be given by the parish priest; such sins were reserved for the bishop; and only from the bishop could the penitent be absolved. For the penitent guilty of still other exceptional sins there was no other course but to seek absolution in person from the pope in Rome. Apostasy from the Catholic faith and profession of the Mohammedan creed was one of the mortal sins not to be pardoned by any one less than the pope. Under pressure in captivity Christian men did lapse in the crusades, and the shame of the surrender, accounted a base betrayal of the cross of Christ, fell on the whole Christian community. Any man released from captivity and known to have lapsed was shunned as a coward and deserter; not to be received into Christian fellowship until he had gone on pilgrimage to Rome and the pope had pardoned him.

The Jewish Question

Christian men in every city in Europe likely to borrow money from their Jewish neighbours hated the Jew for lending it; hated being beholden to the Jew, hated being called upon to pay back the loan with interest. Men going on crusade raised money on the security of their lands to find themselves landless in the end, tenant occupiers where formerly they were landlords.

It is an old story, the resort to the money-lender, the sinking into deeper indebtedness, the hopeless insolvency.

Resentment against the Jewish money-lender was embittered when debtors drifted into poverty and creditors flourished. To make matters worse in certain cities the baser kind of Jews openly mocked at Christians keeping Good Friday; which provoked retaliation and riots ensued. The Council could not stop Christians from borrowing money from Jews, the impecunious can rarely be persuaded not to borrow money for relief of present embarrassment. Bishops and abbots with a laudable desire to build to the glory of God went to the Jews for financial help. The Jews were not the only money-lenders but more conspicuously than Christians they made money-lending their business. Rates of interest must therefore be fixed, the Council decreed.

Mixed marriages of Christian with Jew or with Saracen, Mohammedan, or pagan were another source of trouble in southern Europe. For Catholics to contract a Christian marriage outside the Church was not possible. Hence the canon of the Council requiring all Jews and Saracens to wear a dress distinctive of their race and religion in order that no longer could a mixed marriage be contracted in ignorance of the religious disability. At Passiontide, for the keeping of peace, all Jews must remain within doors. These laws were matters for civil governments to enforce. All that the Council could do was to declare the mind of the Church and leave the State to act. But the State acted with no unanimity in the medieval Europe of warring princes. Ghetto and distinctive dress were not the rule in every land. Generally speaking the Jews for their own protection had their special quarters in the cities they inhabited, wore their accustomed dress because they did not wish to be regarded as gentiles, and were as much opposed to mixed marriages as the Council itself.

The growing influence of Jews in political life, their advancement in public office, shocked the Council. Jews and pagans, too, were being elected or promoted to official positions it was noted; an intolerable thing to the Council that Christians in Christian lands should be subject to the enemies of the cross. The State must prohibit every appointment of Jew, Saracen, or pagan to a position of authority. All this legislation concerning Jews and Saracens was in the main but a repetition of the Canons passed by Pope Alexander III's council of 1179. Innocent III, stickler for canon laws that he was, strove not as innovator but as one concerned for the observance of laws already on the statute book of the Catholic Church.

☙ ☙ ☙

It might be inferred from the proceedings of this great council of the Lateran that an appalling corruption infested Catholic life in the Middle Ages. With all these canonical decrees for the reform of ecclesiastical abuses what health, it might be asked, existed in the Church? How could the Catholic faith survive such corruption, the Christian religion endure, when not infrequently bishops themselves openly violated the commandments of God and were, it appeared, no better than the heathen?

But no inference of general corruption must be inferred from the numerous canons of the Council that diagnosed disease and prescribed remedies. Eight hundred bishops and abbots and priors present at the Council bear witness to the good estate of the Church, the burning desire and resolute will to uproot the tares that flourished—as tares and weeds will flourish in every community of faulty human beings—in medieval Christendom. In certain parts of Europe, in southern France in particular and in lands of eastern Europe but recently brought to the knowledge of the truth, certain bishops and higher clergy fell very far short of the Christian standard of conduct, while parish clergy and laity erred as often as not in sheer ignorance of the commandments they transgressed.

The evil-doer is commonly notorious, the holy and humble of heart are content to live without recognition, happy in their obscurity. Humility is not "news." "Sin in some shape or other is the great staple of history and the sole subject of law." Prelates of ill-regulated life, clerks and laymen addicted to avarice, could not escape attention, their misdeeds were plain for all to see. Nor did they seek to disguise their offences with any cloak of hypocrisy. The sin was rank enough, there was no concealment, no pretence of ethical uprightness on the part of these unworthy members of the body of Christ.

The decrees and canons of the greatest Church Council of the Middle Ages must be read as the sign of a quickened conscience in Christendom, not as a proof of general depravity. A nation or smaller civic community that passes enactments for the checking of avarice or the prohibition of other evil-doing is not sunk in vice. Far from it. It is alive to the disease that troubles its peace, aware that unchecked the disease may spread to the ruin of the whole society, and is resolved that corruption must be got rid of for the sake of the health of the whole.

The seventy-two canons of the Council of Innocent III reveal how very much alive were the pope and council to the numerous offences that plagued all Christendom, offences small and great that, left uncorrected, brought disaster. Not without blemish was the Christian Church in any age—for "the Kingdom of Heaven is like unto a net"—but when all allowance is made for the natural frailty of man there are wrongs intolerable, sins that disgrace and put to shame the fellowship of Christ and call for action. Innocent and his council were the spokesmen of the Christian conscience. They saw and suffered from the evils around them and did their best by canons and decrees to put a stop to the practices of evil-doers. A minority were the evil-doers but a minority that wrought mischief, a minority that unchecked would spread infection. A minority that must be brought to repentance and amendment or utterly cast out. Cut off as a limb diseased must be amputated lest the whole body perish.

⚜ ⚜ ⚜

The decrees of the Council for the most part belong to their age and the age did not welcome discipline. Authority in Church and state was unzealous to enforce laws that rebuked lax morals in high places. Canon law ignored by civil and ecclesiastical authority remained a dead letter in more than one diocese. Only when Church and state cooperated was it effective.

But in two respects the work of the council is alive throughout the Catholic Church to-day.

That very definitive word *transubstantiation* gave the dogma of the Real Presence of Christ in the sacrament of the Holy Eucharist a permanent and protective explanation. By proclaiming the standard of faith for simple and lettered alike it did all that could be done for the apprehension of so profound a mystery. In the centuries to come, in the time we call the Reformation, with divisions and separations that rent beyond repair the Catholic Christendom of the Middle Ages, it was the doctrine of transubstantiation, the doctrine of the Mass, that all Protestants of every church, sect, and denomination most emphatically repudiated. Lutheran, Anglican, Calvinist agreed at least in this that transubstantiation was no doctrine for the members of reformed churches. The Church of England, in its thirty-nine articles, dismissed transubstantiation as "plainly repugnant to the words of Scripture," and has never revoked that opinion. No common eucharistic doctrine unites the members of the various Protestant churches. There is no alternative to transubstantiation, only a variety of beliefs; since Christian people separated from Catholic unity—save the Society of Friends and the Salvation Army—desire to commemorate the Supper of the Lord each in their own way. Transubstantiation is for Catholics the definition of the doctrine of the Real Presence that the Council of the Lateran, divinely guided, gave to the Church in 1215.

The rule of the Council that all Catholics must once a year at least, and that at Easter time, make confession of sins to a priest and receive the Holy Communion is still a precept that must be obeyed under pain of mortal sin. And the seal of the confessional remains more severely unbroken because at that same council it was once and for all time decreed that priests must keep silence concerning sins confessed.

So it is that Innocent's great council touches the spiritual life of Catholics in every land to-day. Across the centuries the doctrine of the Mass, revealed as transubstantiation, is the faith of Catholics, our Easter "duty" the universal obligation.

Fourth General Council of the Lateran

CHAPTER XI
The Passing of Pope Innocent

THE Lateran Council over, its members dispersed, Innocent stayed in Rome till the spring of 1216. In April he set out northward on his last journey, a journey planned to make peace between the warring communities of Pisa and Genoa, to turn these pugnacious and highly prosperous city states from mutual destruction and persuade them to a common cause—the crusade. Innocent went slowly—he was a tired man—lingering in Viterbo, and at Orvieto where he consecrated an altar, and arriving at Perugia towards the end of May. There in Perugia, lifting up his eyes to the hills, seeking in that high Umbrian country with the mountains standing round, fresh health and strength, Innocent waited. But at Perugia the end of the journey had come. The pope's long day's work was done. No more letters would be written. Fever, tertian fever, possessed him. For a while he rallied, eating many oranges every day according to his custom. Then came relapse and a stroke of paralysis. Surgeons bled him but the treatment brought no relief. (Later writers maintained that the news that the dauphin Prince Louis of France had invaded England to depose John excited the sick pontiff—for John was Innocent's vassal—and the excitement was fatal. Which may, or may not be true.) He sank into a state of semiconsciousness, prepared to die and undismayed.

198   Pope Innocent III and His Times

Death came to Innocent III on July 16, a.d. 1216. He was then in his fifty-sixth year and in the nineteenth year of his pontificate. On the night he died Innocent's body was left through carelessness unwatched and thieves broke in and robbed the dead man of the vestments that clothed him, so that on the next morning the corps of the chief shepherd of Christendom was found almost naked. For all that he had done for law and good order in Europe while living, in death theft had the last word.

The funeral rites were celebrated on the following day with all the solemnity due to the dead pontiff, and in the cathedral of St. Lawrence in Perugia the body of Innocent III was laid to rest in a marble sarcophagus. In the same tomb were laid the bodies of two later popes of the thirteenth century, Urban IV (*obiit* 1264) and Martin IV (*obiit* 1285). A plain inscription on the poor and very unworthy monument in the chapel of St. Stephen in the new cathedral at Perugia, erected in the fifteenth century, states that the bones of three Roman pontiffs who died in Perugia were translated to their final resting place in 1615.[30]

Centuries went by. Not till Cardinal Joachim Pecci, sometime bishop of Perugia, became Pope Leo XIII was any memorial to be seen in Rome of the greatest pontiff of the Middle Ages. Leo XIII, pre-eminently Innocent's disciple, had the statesman's mind, the Christian statesman's outlook. He it was who bade the Catholics of France accept the republic and

---

[30]

Ossa
Trium Romanorum Pontificum
Qui Perusiae Obierunt
Innocen. III Urban IV Mart. IV
A.MCCXVI. A.MCCLXIV. A.MCCLXXXV.

Ab Hujus Templi Sacrario
Huc Translata
Anno MDCXV

abandon royalist intrigues; who saw the social question in its gravity and gave to the world the famous encyclical *Rerum et Novarum*. Leo XIII shared Innocent's love of letters and classical scholarship. It was appropriate that he should order a monument to be set up, a.d. 1891, in the basilica of St. John Lateran to his great predecessor.

⚜ ⚜ ⚜

With the passing of Innocent III passed the fullness of papal power and papal influence in Europe. In the century after Innocent's death sixteen popes reigned; for the most part pontiffs of ability and all of good character, but lacking the personality and statesmanship of Innocent III. Tormented by the amazing Hohenstaufen emperor, Frederick II, distracted by the rivalries of Roman cardinals, vainly in that thirteenth century did other popes seek to exert the authority of Innocent III. In a time of political despair a hermit of the Abruzzi, famed in southern Italy for his holy life, totally inexperienced in statecraft, to be known as San Celestino, St. Celestine, was drawn from the solitude he loved, by the appeal of kings and cardinals, that they might end the two years interregnum. So hopeless it appeared for the cardinals—there were but eleven—to come to an agreement; so scandalous the vacancy of the Holy See! But the burden was too heavy for Celestine V. He never reached Rome, never indeed got beyond Naples and the custody of its king. After a few months of ineffectual grappling with responsibility that was altogether too much for him, Celestine abdicated and fled to his solitude — only to be held in captivity by his successor, Boniface VIII, who feared a schism.

With the tragedy of Boniface VIII the decline of the medieval papacy is evident. Boniface would have ruled as

Innocent ruled. He had the strong will, the stature and bodily strength of a man born to rule. Also he had the vision of a united Christendom: all princes, vassals of the Holy See, at peace with one another and at war with the forces of Islam for the recovery of Palestine. Strength and vision were not enough. The pride of Boniface was more than enough. He had neither the profound spiritual life of Innocent, nor the patience. Neither had Boniface that sympathetic knowledge of men that Innocent, with his large heart, possessed. Boniface thundered and issued bulls that demanded obedience from kings; the kings ignored and defied him. In the end his excommunication of Philip the Fair of France, with whom he had long been at enmity, brought doom. Boniface, undefended in his own palace in Anagni when the French privy councillor Nogaret forced an entrance, assaulted by a cardinal of the Colonna family, lived but a month after the outrage. He had done no more than reassert the feudal claims of Innocent, but in his pride and violence without due charity the claims were utterly rejected. Feudalism itself was no longer of general acceptance. A year after the death of Boniface, in 1303, a Gascon, archbishop of Bordeaux, was elected pope, and with his residence at Avignon, Rome forsaken, began the seventy years of Babylonian exile.

The papacy, sunk in forty years of the great schism, with the faithful divided in their allegiance, would sink still lower under Renaissance popes in love with the glories of the world, contending in arms for political power, reducing the Vicar of Christ to the position of a lesser European prince. When that uncompromising Dominican friar, Pope St. Pius V, excommunicated Elizabeth, the sentence brought affliction on English Catholics but no political hurt to the English queen. The day of papal excommunication of recalcitrant sovereigns was long past. No matter how great the provocation no ruler after the reign of Pius V would be excommunicated by the pope. (Yet Pope Gregory in a papal brief to Fitzmaurice, commending the invasion of Ireland in 1577, but in ignorance of the real balance of forces and the chance of success, certainly favoured the forcible deposition of Elizabeth whom he described as "the enemy of God and man.")

The vision of pope and emperor guiding the destinies of Christian and Catholic Europe, wielding the two swords—the pope the spiritual, the emperor the political—dissolved in the thirteenth century. Yet much of Innocent's influence survived and bore abundant fruit in that same ever memorable century. His discernment of the spiritual genius of St. Dominic and St. Francis, his quick perception of the saving work to be done by the orders of friars in their respective fields, was richly justified when the intellectual revival of the twelfth century flowered in its fullness; with St. Albert the Great and St. Thomas Aquinas shaping Catholic philosophy and St. Bonaventura, the Franciscan doctor, approaching truth from another angle not less profound.

We are here in the period of university foundation, the middle ages of the thirteenth and fourteenth centuries. Oxford has its students housed within colleges: University, Merton, Balliol, with Gloucester Hall—the Worcester of our time—as a residence for Benedictine monks. All these are of thirteenth-century foundation. In Italy, we have the Universities of Rome, Perugia, and Florence; in France, the University of Grenoble; in Bohemia, the University of Prague; in the Empire, the Universities of Vienna and Heidelberg; in Poland, the University of Cracow—all universities founded in medieval Europe. The Middle Ages are closing with the fifteenth century when the Universities of Turin; of St. Andrews, Glasgow, and Aberdeen in Scotland; of Barcelona and Valencia in Spain; of Leipzig, Basel, Mainz, Tubingen, Upsala, and Copenhagen are being established. And here the New World, whither the Church had already carried civilisation, takes up the flaming torch. In North and South America universities quickly arise. So in the sixteenth century, Mexico claims its flourishing and well-standardised Catholic University, although not until the eighteenth century will the United States follow with Harvard University, and not until the nineteenth will England enjoy other universities than Oxford and Cambridge.

Pope Innocent III gave to scholarship the encouragement needed, assisted the impetus to learning that produced universities. He could ensure no escape from failure in any institutions of mankind. The history of university usefulness tells of repeated fluctuations, depressions, revivals, forsaken ideals, standards of learning lowered: melancholy features inevitable in the best of human devices.

The Renaissance, with its humanism that, except in England, was largely pagan, would hasten forgetfulness of the neglected Catholic philosophy of the medieval doctors. The Reformation, sundering the unity of Christendom beyond repair, would for a time make an end of all free theological discussion. The *Aufklärung* of the eighteenth century, hailed as the dawn of man's complete emancipation from the dogma of revealed religion, would land the world in such a mess of fantastic, violent assertion, such a carnival of unreason, that as the dusk descends on the murky day of liberal "enlightenment" many are to be troubled with the doubt whether any vestige of Christian civilisation can survive in Europe.

Secular liberalism holding aloof from divine guidance, distrusting all approach to truth in revealed religion, satisfied that man is able to find his way to higher things by inner light alone, positive that Catholic faith and Christian religion are indeed unnecessary for "progressive" minds, can but survey the world it has produced, the society it has begotten, and in the distress of nations wonder what will happen next.

Sed nondum finis est: "the end is not yet." To the Catholic philosophy of St. Thomas—its revival instigated by Pope Leo XIII, fostered by his successors in the Holy See—clergy and laity, men and women alike, have turned in numbers that daily increase. The emptiness of philosophies that ignore or deny the revelation of God and His abiding presence in the world is confessed. All things true, noble, and of good report in the liberal and democratic ideal are seen contained in Catholic philosophy.

From the Vatican in the twentieth century the Vicar of Christ, chief shepherd of the souls of men, proclaims, as did Innocent III in his day, to all who heed the message, that in following the commandments of God are justice and peace assured; that in Christ is revealed, while time shall last, the Way, the Truth, and the Life. Men stumble in darkness, choosing often unwittingly darkness rather than light. They stumbled in the Middle Ages, rejecting the wise counsels of Pope Innocent III, while the rulers of this world brought misery untold to multitudes. Rejecting the wise counsels that come from the Vatican, despising authority other than their own wayward wills, men and their rulers stumble today and the distress of nations is acute. The witness of the Catholic Church remains—in the knowledge of God is eternal life. The unsilenced voice of the supreme head of the Church on earth still warns mankind of judgement, still bids us return to the paths of peace and the doing of justice. Darkness or light? The choice is for every man in every age. Pope Innocent passed from the world, as all must pass. The wisdom Innocent taught, in word and in life, has not passed; for it belongs to the order of God, imperishable, immortal.

❧ Finis ❧

Table of Dates

Papacy	Empire	England	France
	1154-1190 Frederick I Barbarosa	1154-1189 Henry II	
1159 Alexander III			
1160 Lothario Conti		1170 Murder of St. Thomas Becket	
1179 Third Gen. Council of the Lateran			1180-1223 Philip Augustus
1181 Lucius III			
1185 Urban III			
1187 Gregory VIII			
1187 Clement III		1189-1199 Richard I, Coeur de Leon	
1191 Celestine III	1190-1197 Henry IV		
1198 Innocent III	1198-1214 Otto of Brunswick	1199-1216 John	1203 Fourth Crusade
	1198-1208 Philip of Swabia		1204 Latin Empire of Constantinople
1215 Fourth Gen. Council of the Lateran		1215 Magna Charta	
1216 Honorius III	1215-1250 Frederick II		

Notes on Authorities

Migne, *Patrologia Latina*, 4 volumes — containing more than 4000 letters, sermons, and other documents from the papal registers.

Luchaire, A., *Innocent III*, 6 volumes (Paris, 1904). The fullest and most complete biography.

Mann, H. K., *Lives of the Popes,* volumes XI and XII Innocent III (London, 1915).

Other books, that should be useful to the general reader and to the student, are named in footnotes.

Other Books from Mediatrix Press

Rome and the Counter-Reformation in England
Philip Hughes
With a New Foreword by Charles A. Coulombe

The Life of St. Francis of Assisi
Candide Challipe, OFM
Translated by the Oratorians of London

The Life of St. Philip Neri
Anne Hope

The Life of Cesar Cardinal Baronius
Amabel Kerr

*The True Story of the Sword in the Stone:
A Compendium on the life of St. Galgano*
Torchij dei Gaius Geletti
Translated by Ryan Grant

St. Thérèse and the Faithful
Benedict Williamson

A Small Catechism for Catholics
St. Peter Canisius, S.J.

On the Roman Pontiff
St. Robert Bellarmine

On the Marks of the Church
St. Robert Bellarmine

On the Church Militant
St. Robert Bellarmine

The Work of Theology
Francisco Muñiz, O.P.

The Franciscan Way of the Cross
Latin-English

Printed in Great Britain
by Amazon